Hetty Green

The First Lady

of Wall Street

"Some young women do better in business than men."

Hetty Green (1834 – 1916)

First published November 2019

by Spiramus Press Ltd
102 Blandford Street
London W1U 8AG

Telephone +44 20 7224 0080

www.spiramus.com

© Spiramus Press Ltd

ISBN

9781910151747 Paperback

9781910151754 Digital

British Library Cataloguing-in-Publication Data.

A catalogue record for this book is available from the British Library.

The right of Wyn Derbyshire to be identified as the author of this work has been asserted by him in accordance with the Copyright, Designs and Patents Act, 1988.

Printed and bound in the US by IPG

For Judith and Michael Neal

Contents

Introduction

Hetty Howland Green, born Hetty Howland Robinson, and known in her later years as "The Witch of Wall Street", was born on 21st November 1834 at her parents' home in the whaling town of New Bedford, Massachusetts. Her parents were both Quakers and many of the traditional values commonly attributed to Quaker teachings, such as thrift, hard work, diligence and honesty, coupled with other, less easily attributable qualities such as icy determination, frequent stubbornness, a need for privacy and a self-reliance which seemed at times to border on the pathological, were later cited by many commentators as the reason for Hetty Green's extraordinary ascent up the pyramid of wealth to a point where, in the earliest years of the twentieth century, she was being identified as the richest woman in America. At the same time, many were also decrying her for being, as they saw it, cold and unfeeling, even towards members of her own family, and possessing a love of money which went far beyond simple avarice and well into penny-pinching madness. When in later years, the story was put about that she had refused to pay the medical bills of her son for much needed treatment of a damaged leg, leaving him nearly crippled for life, it was believed in many quarters, and held up as yet another example of her meanness and inhumanity, ready belief in the story being eased by the steadfast refusal of Hetty (or indeed, her son) to comment on, or otherwise respond publicly to the allegations.

As is often the case however, the public of the time, and indeed ever since, were responding to and to a large extent judging a caricature image of a person in the public eye, rather than the actual person under consideration. Hetty's public image, in later years at least, possessed some elements of her true nature, but it omitted many important aspects that were obscure (or in some cases, even deliberately opaque, rendered so not least by Hetty herself, for reasons of her own). She was certainly no saint (as she herself would have been among the first to admit, though perhaps not the very first) but nor was she a financial demoness. She probably was, however, in her day the richest woman in America, and possibly in the world, possessing when she died a personal fortune of at least $100 million,[1] most of which she had accumulated by herself. That she should have achieved so much in financial terms at a time when the laws and customs of the country made it difficult indeed for a woman to function in business at all was and is remarkable. Perhaps even more so however is that unlike most of the male financial magnates who were her contemporaries, or nearly so – men such as John D Rockefeller, Andrew Carnegie and J P Morgan for instance – she did not focus upon one area of endeavour, whether it be a particular aspect of industry such as oil, steel or chemicals, or as in the case of Morgan, finance itself, ending up to a very large extent dominating a specific field of activity, and acquiring great personal wealth in the process. Rather, Hetty's fortune primarily came from a series of careful and shrewd investment steps – a mortgage here, a foreclosure there, loaning money to carefully chosen borrowers and claiming the resulting interest, making thoughtful acquisitions of stakes in publicly-traded companies and so on. This approach requires skills such as an insightful judgment of situations and people, and background knowledge of how businesses operate and the dangers they can face. It also requires patience and the possession of at least some initial nugget of capital – seed money that can be used to kick-start the investment journey. Some of the skills she needed and used to build her fortune Hetty may have possessed from birth. As for others, such as the core knowledge which enabled her to operate in the financial and business world, and importantly, the seed money she would so successfully multiply over and over again in the decades to come, these were acquired by Hetty

---

[1] Approximately $2 billion today.

during her childhood and the years of her early adulthood, and she acquired them principally from her family.

Hetty's seed money, without which she almost certainly would not have managed to accumulate the bulk of her fortune, essentially came from two sources, both by way of inheritance, specifically legacies from her father and her aunt. Although in both cases, her freedom to control those legacies was more constrained than she had hoped, thanks primarily to the creation of trusts (which she challenged but largely to no avail), by her early thirties she was a millionairess in her own right, and shortly after receiving those legacies she married a man who was also a millionaire (though admittedly he would lose most of his fortune over the course of his life). Hetty could have lived a comfortable, even luxurious, life if she had simply placed the money she inherited in a few carefully selected and safe investments and chosen to live off the resulting dividends and interest. The question therefore arises as to why she did not do this, and instead devoted most of her life in seeking to multiply her initial fortune many times over, a task at which she succeeded to a greater extent than perhaps even she could have envisaged when she began her investing career in earnest.

This is a question which is easy to pose but harder to answer with any certainty. One thing appears clear from an examination of her life – she did not expand her fortune simply so she could enjoy material possessions. Hetty's reputation as being a woman who disdained extravagance and ostentatious living was and is well founded on fact; if anything, she went too far in her abstemiousness, certainly as far as clothing, housing and the feeding of herself were concerned. Purchasing a few extra dresses would not have stretched her finances unduly.

It seems likely that there was a combination of factors and circumstances which led Hetty to build her fortune as she did. These included her being born into a family which over the previous few generations had already accumulated significant wealth and in which there was a considerable tradition of what we would now call entrepreneurialism. Then too there was the fact that she was an only child, raised to understand basic financial principles and to see herself as the heiress of the family, yet having no significant wealth of her own before her father died in 1865. When at last she received her seed money, she was determined to put the principles she had learned into practice and this is precisely what she did. That she was female too was almost certainly a factor; at that time and place there was no realistic prospect of her pursuing any form of career out in the wider world and yet her life shows she had a strong need to be independent and self-sufficient, particularly in financial matters, and particularly after events occurred which led her to conclude that her husband simply could not be trusted to safeguard her money as well as she could do herself. Given these factors and circumstances, it is unsurprising that Hetty devoted so much of her time to developing her own financial interests; for her, apart from her parental responsibilities (which she did take seriously, albeit it in her own idiosyncratic and occasionally unorthodox ways) there was in fact little else for her to do or that she wished to do. As far as Hetty was concerned, her growing fortune served to guarantee her own independence, and this was something she cherished, and needed, ever more as the years went by. That fortune also served as a form of protection for her own immediate family, at least her son and daughter, and even her husband to an extent, and that too was something that was important to her. It also effectively ensured she dominated many of those around her and this also was not something to which she objected.

As previously noted, unlike many of the tycoons of her day, Hetty did not create vast new industries, or play a significant role in world events. The bulk of her fortune ultimately but quietly found its way into the coffers of various charities and she left no monuments to her memory such as the palatial mansions of the Vanderbilts or the well-endowed educational institutions of Andrew Carnegie. Instead, Hetty's life itself stands as her memorial, an example (admittedly a rare one) of a woman of the Victorian era steadily, methodically, even sometimes stubbornly, creating a multimillion dollar fortune regardless of the views of others, and doing so in a world where many would have thought such a feat impossible, at least before Hetty achieved it. It must be admitted she could on occasions be tough and brusque in her business dealings with others, and indeed sometimes within the scope of her personal life. That she had idiosyncratic, possibly eccentric, and on occasions perhaps even undesirable, aspects of her personality also cannot be denied. That she serves as one of the most fascinating examples of a wealth accumulator in all of financial history seems beyond question.

Wyn Derbyshire

St Albans, August 2019

Early Years

Hetty's father, Edward Mott Robinson, was born on 8th January 1800. He came from a prominent Quaker family based in Philadelphia, but with historic roots leading back to Rhode Island, where one of his ancestors had been a Deputy Governor during the colonial period. Freely admitting a deep desire to accumulate a fortune, he had started his business career working with his brother William in a wool and cotton manufacturing business, but had soon branched out on his own account into the oil industry, which at that time was based almost exclusively on whaling. In his early thirties, he had moved to New Bedford, then one of the most important centres of the whaling industry, in search of business opportunities.

For a person eager to accumulate wealth, New Bedford in the 1830s was a good place to be. Whaling itself, and the rendering of whales into commercially useful commodities, such as oil and other vital resources such as ambergris,[2] was dirty, hard, unpleasant and frequently dangerous work, both at sea and on land, but those products were desperately needed not only by the rapidly expanding industries of the United States, but also those of further afield, such as those in Great Britain. Oil from whales helped to keep the wheels in the world's earliest industrial centres turning, and there being no realistic alternative at that time, demand for whale oil was soaring year by year, something that would continue until underground oil reserves began to be exploited in 1859 and the years that immediately followed. Such ever increasing demand led to the boom years of the whaling industry, and the resulting revenues enriched not only the individuals and businesses creating that wealth, but also the towns in which they were based. New

---

[2] A wax derived from sperm whale intestines and used in the production of perfume.

Bedford as seen by Edward Robinson when he first moved there in 1833 must in some ways have been a strange place to see, a bustling, busy port, with crowded wharves and warehouses, busy offices and shops, interspersed with sleazy bars, run-down boarding houses and brothels. Yet at the same time, in more favoured areas, it presented the façade of a dignified, relatively sophisticated and prosperous community, one placing an emphasis on civic developments such as well paved streets (in some quarters at least), street lighting (rare for the time) and other amenities such as well-stocked public libraries, meeting halls and schools, civic improvements made possible by the local taxes generated by the whaling and associated businesses. This general perspective of prosperity was enhanced in the better parts of the town by the presence of the houses of the wealthy, mostly whaling magnates and other successful business owners, who had built for themselves homes that Herman Melville, author of Moby Dick and a man who knew New Bedford well, did not hesitate to describe as being "patrician-like". It is not surprising that Edward Robinson rapidly concluded that this was a place where he could build his fortune.

Key to the making of that fortune (and thus to Hetty's subsequent, greater one) was Edward's encounter with the Howland family. The Howlands, also of Quaker stock, had been amongst the first English settlers in the New World – one member of the family had arrived on the _Mayflower_[3] – others arrived on ships which had followed shortly thereafter – and the family had long since been involved in various aspects of the sea trade. During the last years of the eighteenth century, one member of the family, Isaac Howland Jr. (born in 1755) had migrated to New Bedford and set up a merchant shipping business

---

[3] Although he nearly didn't – this was John Howland, who during the voyage of the _Mayflower_, managed to fall overboard during a storm, but succeeded in grabbing and holding on to a halyard, until he could be rescued by members of the crew.

there which became known as Isaac Howland Jr. and Company and prospered. By the time of the Battle of Waterloo in 1815, whaling was becoming a significant part of the New Bedford economy, and the attractions of the port began to tempt whalers away from Nantucket, originally the principal centre of the industry, but which possessed too shallow a harbour for use by the newer, larger whaling vessels which were then being introduced. Always alert to new potential sources of profit, Isaac began around this time to invest in whaling ships and to underwrite whaling voyages which could span the world and take years to complete. He also began to invest in banking and money-lending ventures, as well as in insurance. Within a few years, Isaac's businesses, both on land and at sea, had made him a very wealthy man and the Howlands one of the principal Quaker families of the town.

By the time of Edward Robinson's arrival in New Bedford, in 1833, Isaac's son-in-law Gideon Howland Jr.[4] either had assumed or was in the process of assuming responsibility for the day-to-day running of Isaac Howland Jr. and Company. Gideon had married Isaac's daughter Mehitable, who was his second cousin, in 1798, and she had presented him with two daughters, first Sylvia Ann in 1806, who had been born with spinal problems and remained physically weak, almost a semi-invalid, all of her life and then Abby Slocum, who was born in 1809. Six months or so after Abby's birth, Mehitable had died, and the newly widowed Gideon and his two young daughters had moved into Isaac's house. It became their family home, and they continued to share it with Ruth, Isaac's second wife, after Isaac's death.[5]

Being a Quaker himself, it is perhaps not surprising that shortly after arriving in New Bedford, Edward Robinson seems to have made the acquaintance of the Howlands. By the time of his arrival, Sylvia and Abby were both of an age when marriage was a matter to be considered

---

[4] And also another member of the extended Howland clan.
[5] Isaac's first wife, Abigail, died in 1814.

seriously (indeed, they had been for several years), and this was especially so for them as it was well known they were the ultimate heiresses to Isaac's fortune, now estimated to exceed a quarter of a million dollars, a significant sum for the time, equivalent to about \$7.4 million today. Edward himself would have been well aware of the financial prospects of both daughters. He seems to have shown little or no interest in Sylvia, who even in her mid to late twenties was acquiring a reputation of being sharp-tongued and someone sometimes difficult to deal with, but Abby was a different prospect entirely, and Edward promptly began to court her within the customs of the Quaker community. Abby appears to have welcomed his interest, but Sylvia, no doubt jealous of the attentions being paid to her younger, physically more able sister rapidly came to resent him in a quietly seething fashion, a state of affairs which was to continue for the rest of their days.

Edward and Abby were married on 29th December 1833, and the financial wisdom of the marriage manifested itself two weeks later when on 12th January 1834, Isaac Howland Jr. died, leaving approximately \$130,000 (\$3.8 million today) to each of his granddaughters. Of Abby's share of this inheritance, Edward now assumed control of \$90,000, whilst another partner in the firm, Thomas Mandell held the balance of \$40,000 on behalf of Abby as her trustee. Mandell also held a portion of Sylvia's share on trust for her, and soon slipped into the role as family confidant and general financial adviser. For his part, Edward was now well on his way to achieving his goal of becoming a wealthy man[6], and Abby's discovery that she was pregnant a few months after their marriage led him to conclude that he was also about to gain an heir. He was nearly right, but when Abby gave birth on

---

[6] A process that would be further enhanced in 1847 when Gideon died, also leaving the bulk of his fortune to Abby and Sylvia. Edward used Abby's share of the inheritance to seize effective control of Isaac Howland Jr. and Company; before long, he was being described by one New Bedford resident as "the very Napoleon of our little business community" – it was meant as praise.

21st November 1834, she did so to Edward's heiress rather than his heir, producing a daughter whom her parents would name Hetty Howland Robinson. Edward may have been disappointed at having been denied a son, but he threw himself into developing the family businesses, which he did with considerable success, as well as moving his family into a new and imposing mansion intended to serve as a beacon to highlight the family's financial success. Hetty herself spent little time in that house however, as within a few months Abby was pregnant again, and it was decided that Hetty should move to live with her grandfather Gideon, who was still sharing a house with Sylvia and Isaac's widow Ruth. Hetty would henceforth spend much of her childhood either living in her grandfather's house, or in another property called Round Hill in Dartmouth, Massachusetts, some eight miles or so from New Bedford and which had been owned by the Howland family for several generations.

On 20th May 1836, Abby gave birth to a boy whom she and Edward named Isaac Howland Robinson, but he was frail, and died a few months later. Moreover, the process of childbirth had so weakened Abby physically and emotionally that she was unable to have any further children. To make matters even worse, the trauma of the birth and death of the infant Isaac drove a wedge between Edward and Abby. They were never emotionally or physically close again, and so far as Hetty was concerned, from that time on, Abby would play only a small role in her life. As for her father, she would in many ways become very close to him albeit that she also only saw him intermittently.

With the loss of his son and the effective failure of his marriage, Edward devoted himself even more to the business of making money, and the importance of money and the need to build and protect the family fortune were concepts which the young Hetty rapidly incorporated into her own character and values. There were probably several reasons for this, not least the desire to please and earn the respect of her father, who in many ways would be one of the very few males that Hetty showed any sign of wishing to impress. She early learned the virtues of thrift and saving (she was after all being raised within a family and social circle which still identified strongly with Quaker traditional values), and early began to save much of her allowance in her first bank account, rather than spend it as other children might have been tempted so to do. Then too as she grew older, she became acutely aware of her position not only as heiress to the Robinson fortune, but also (probably) to the balance of the Howland fortune still effectively under the control of her aunt Sylvia. Some effort was made by the family to prepare her for the financial responsibilities it was anticipated she might one day face. Her first lessons were given to her by a tutor and she rapidly learned to read and write (though her spelling often left much to be desired), and soon could carry out basic arithmetic calculations. Numbers and letters mastered, she was asked to read financial news reports to her grandfather Gideon and her father, as both of them suffered from failing eyesight as they grew older and increasingly relied on young Hetty to fulfil this chore. This in turn led her, as she herself would later state "to know what stocks and bonds were, how the markets fluctuated and the meaning of 'bulls' and 'bears'". Her father also began, at first perhaps only tentatively, to involve her in his day-to-day business activities. Not only, once she had grown old enough, did he begin to take her along sometimes as he went about his rounds of the various businesses in New Bedford, but he also began to discuss business reports with her and describe his business activities, taking pains as she herself later noted to "carefully explain to [her] those things [she] did not understand". She was required to keep accounts of her own savings and expenditures, an experience which she found invaluable, commenting later in life that it was the best sort of training, since it led to the habit of keeping track of every cent spent or saved, and getting the best value for any money spent.

As regards more traditional forms of education, Hetty twice went away to boarding schools, the first time at the age of eleven when she was sent to a Quaker school in Sandwich, Massachusetts run by a headmistress called Eliza Wing. By all accounts it was a dour, dreary establishment, concentrating primarily on teaching a narrow religious syllabus and very little else, and on the provision of tasteless basic meals for the children which Hetty learned to choke down but never grew to like. She endured the regime there for nearly five years, and then when she was fifteen, she was despatched to the Friends Academy, a Quaker school in New Bedford, where there was a greater emphasis on academic teachings in areas such as literature and science. Hetty spent two years there, but showed little sign of benefiting from the change of educational regime. Family members commented regularly on her poor spelling, lack of apparent refinement and generally shabby appearance, the latter two aspects in particular seeming to upset her aunt Sylvia, who had very definite views about the role of females, and especially how they should be educated and the way they should deport themselves, not least as a means of attracting suitable husbands, a matter Sylvia considered very important given Hetty's status as the ultimate heiress to the family fortunes. To Sylvia's eyes, her niece required some polishing of her character and manners, and Hetty's apparent lack of interest in more traditional feminine pursuits was something to be deplored. To address these perceived faults, Sylvia persuaded other members of the family that Hetty would benefit from attending a finishing school she knew of in Boston. Established by Anna Cabot Lowell, the school's emphasis was on training girls to be socially acceptable young ladies, well-read in the mainstream literature of the day, skilled with pen and needle and musical instruments, confident in their abilities one day to run their own household establishments and possessing the social graces that would enable them to flourish in the salons, dining rooms and ballrooms of Boston, New York and further afield, surrounded by other members of their financially-advantaged class. It was a quite a departure from the traditional Quaker values of the family, but the family was persuaded, and Hetty was despatched to attend the school when she was seventeen.

She spent nearly three years at the school, and appears to have picked up enough of the social graces to at least partially placate the demands of Sylvia, though she also now was in the process of developing a reputation of being able to unleash temper tantrums when she perceived any slights against herself. Hetty certainly learned to dance, for she mentioned in later years of attending balls given in honour of various visiting dignitaries (and at one of them given in 1860, of dancing with the Prince of Wales who was visiting the United States at the time). In fact, by the time she left the school, she had acquired sufficient social grace to permit her to move confidently within upper class society when and as she wished, though always (as would become apparent) on her own terms.

Shortly after leaving school, and principally at the behest (once again) of Sylvia, but also with the specific approval of her father (who gave her $1200 to enable her to buy herself fashionable clothes and other accoutrements), she was despatched to New York to spend some time with Henry and Sarah Grinnell and their family. Henry was Hetty's mother's cousin, and the Grinnells, wealthy and well-connected in their own right, took upon themselves the role of introducing Hetty into New York society, at least partly with the aim of ensuring that any young men that Hetty might meet would be suitable potential spouses. But whilst many young women of her time and class devoted much of their time in New York and other centres of fashionable society to the very specific mission of finding acceptable, that is to say, wealthy and preferably socially well-connected husbands, Hetty seems to have remained free of such ambitions, and indeed to have scorned them. None of the young men she met at this time appear to have interested her romantically, and suddenly losing patience with the whole process, she cut short her visit to New York, and returned home to New Bedford, bringing back with her $1000 worth of bonds which she had purchased out of $1200 that her father had given her for the purchase of fashionable clothes. Fashionable clothes did not interest her, bonds returning a satisfactory rate of interest certainly did. This was probably the first significant investment that Hetty made on her own initiative; the investment apparently did well, and she kept her eyes open for other similar opportunities.

Her father was pleased to see her, accepting her reasons for wanting to return and approving of her bond purchases. Nevertheless, on her permanent return to New Bedford, Hetty found that there had been changes whilst she had been away at school and then in New York. She continued to move back and forth between the house at Round Hill, now under the control of Sylvia, and her father's house in New Bedford, keeping a bedroom in each, much as she had in earlier years. But whilst her father had continued to apply himself to building his business and fortune in her absence,[7] she found her aunt Sylvia, still bitterly resentful of Edward and especially of his apparent usurpation of much of the family's fortune, was rapidly adapting to the life of a rich semi-invalid, gathering around her a growing number of servants and increasingly inclined to live (at least to Hetty's censorious eyes) a life of extravagance. Hetty disapproved even though there was no doubt that Sylvia could easily afford such a lifestyle, and it must also be said that compared to the lifestyles then being adopted by other wealthy people in the United States, Sylvia's taste for "luxury" was modest indeed. There was certainly real affection between Sylvia and Hetty from time to time, but despite this, relations between aunt and niece grew

---

[7] He did so with such success that by the late 1850s, he and Sylvia (whose continuing financial interest in Isaac Howland Jr. and Company meant that Edward's success at building the company had also benefited her) were probably the two richest individuals in New Bedford.

increasingly tense following Hetty's return to New Bedford. This process became more marked as Sylvia's frail health began to worsen, and her need to assert control over others increased, perhaps a subconscious compensation for her increasing physical helplessness. That need to control led to Sylvia expecting total subservience and loyalty from her servants, and their constant attendance upon her and to her wishes.

Sylvia for her part enjoyed a strange love-hate relationship with her niece. On the one hand, she freely gave Hetty a gift of $20,000 and at times openly referred to her as being her heir; at other times, she fiercely criticised Hetty's dress style, her inability (or stubborn refusal) to follow advice when offered (especially when it was offered by Sylvia herself) and Hetty's general standards of behaviour. Hetty in turn was conscious that (notwithstanding her aunt's gift, and her future prospects) she was a virtual pauper compared to her father and mother (who were more estranged from one another than ever) and to her aunt, and as a consequence she was ever more anxious to protect her rights of inheritance, as she saw them, though at this time she had in fact no legal claim on Sylvia's fortune at all. She felt financially vulnerable. She was inclined to see Sylvia's willingness to spend at least some of her money on what Hetty perceived as unnecessary luxuries as a frittering away of Hetty's own future inheritance, and she did not hesitate to let her feelings be known, lecturing her aunt on the dangers of reckless spending. Making matters worse, Sylvia fiercely protected her financial privacy, excluding Hetty from any detailed knowledge of her business affairs, whilst at the same time, her housekeeper and cook Fally Brownell was entrusted with the key to the trunk in which Sylvia kept large quantities of cash, jewels and financial papers. Fally was under strict instructions not to give the key to anyone, especially Hetty, and this exclusion heightened Hetty's fears that one or more of the servants, and particularly Fally, would find some way to take improper advantage of Sylvia's wealth. Hetty did a poor job at hiding her suspicions, and relations between her and her aunt's staff also deteriorated rapidly.[8]

Hetty sought at least some relief from such tensions and difficulties by once again involving herself in her father's business life, something Edward openly encouraged, anxious as he was to ensure that when the time came, Hetty would be well able to shoulder the burden of the Howland fortune. His control of the portion of that fortune not within Sylvia's grasp increased in February 1860, when Abby died, leaving over $128,000. Edward effectively claimed this as his own, causing for a time a distinct cooling of relations between father and daughter, who consulted legal advisers to see if she could force him to disgorge himself of at least some of the wealth he had just acquired. She was unsuccessful; her father did agree to transfer a small house, valued at approximately $8000 into Hetty's name, but he wasn't about to surrender control of the rest of the money. Hetty, apparently defeated for the moment, sought some sort of refuge with her aunt, their ongoing feud momentarily suspended (more or less). Her father seemed unconcerned, and in any event, he was busy. For some time now, he had been increasingly concerned that the best (that is to say, most profitable) days of the whaling industry were fast passing, partly due to the increasing rarity of whales due to over-hunting, and partly due to the discovery of the oil fields of Pennsylvania, which as Edward promptly foresaw sounded the death knell for New England's whaling industry generally. A sharp industrial recession in 1857 had also damaged business confidence, and added to the financial difficulties

---

[8] On one occasion, an altercation between Hetty and Fally reached such a stage of hostility that Hetty pushed the housekeeper hard, resulting in Fally falling down a flight of stairs. Sylvia, furious with Hetty, effectively threatened to disinherit Hetty unless she apologised. Hetty did so but Sylvia still had to pay Fally $1000 as the price for her continuing to work for her. This did nothing to improve the relationship between aunt and niece.

across the United States. The country was also increasingly divided over the issues of slavery and the growing industrial might of the northern states which threatened to supplant the traditional political dominance of the South. Calls for secession from the Union were being heard from many of the southern states in response to this state of affairs, calls which were increasing in intensity (and vitriol) as the likelihood of Abraham Lincoln standing for and winning the Presidency became ever more apparent. Many were now speculating openly about the possibility of civil war, and Edward was not the only businessman anticipating an industrial boom for the North if civil war did erupt.

Determined to ensure he prospered from any such boom, whilst simultaneously seeking to sidestep the inevitable problems that would arise as a consequence of the demise of whaling, Edward Robinson began to sell much of his whaling business, and invested instead in a New York mercantile firm called William T. Coleman and Company which as well as operating a large fleet of merchant ships, also specialised in real estate ventures. He became a partner in the firm, and around the time of President Lincoln's first inauguration on 4th March 1861, announced he would be moving to New York. He asked Hetty if she would like to accompany him, which gave her a dilemma. On the one hand, she would enjoy watching and learning from him as he established himself in New York; on the other, she still felt resentment at the way he had claimed the lion's share of her mother's inheritance, and in addition there was the necessity (as she saw it) of having to keep an eye on her aunt's servants. To be fair to Hetty, she was also concerned about the state of Sylvia's health, which was steadily worsening. Hetty finally decided to move to New York with her father, but returned to New Bedford frequently.

Mr Green

In the summer or autumn of 1860, before the move to New York, Hetty decided it would be advisable to try to regularise her position as Sylvia's heir, partly in order to gain some certainty as to her position as the ultimate beneficiary of the Howland fortune, and partly (no doubt) to seek to avert any attempt by any of Sylvia's servants to claim part of the money for themselves. She approached her aunt, and suggested that they should prepare mutual wills. Although the likelihood of Hetty dying before Sylvia was small, Hetty proposed that her will should provide that her estate should pass to any children of hers living at the date of her death, but if there were no children, the estate would be paid to her aunt's favourite charity. Sylvia appears not to have had any objections to this plan, at least so far as Hetty's will was concerned and a suitable will was drawn up for Hetty, and duly executed on 19th September 1860. That seemed simple enough, but things were a little more complicated as regards the proposed disposal of Sylvia's estate.

As might be expected of a wealthy spinster, Sylvia already had a valid will, one which had been prepared whilst Hetty was at school. Under its terms, two-thirds of Sylvia's money was to have been left to Abby, or if Abby were to die before Sylvia (which she did), then Abby's share was to be received by Hetty. The balance of Sylvia's estate was to be paid to various charities that Sylvia had long supported. However, neither Abby nor Hetty were to receive their full share of the money absolutely; instead two-thirds of their share was to be paid into a trust fund created for the purpose, and that fund would be administered by trustees. Abby (or Hetty) would be entitled to the income from trust fund but would not have access to the capital. This was (and to some extent, still is) a fairly common approach taken by wealthy individuals when settling how their fortunes should be distributed after their deaths, particularly if there were concerns that the prospective recipients of the inherited wealth might mismanage or otherwise squander that wealth once it had been received. Needless to say, Hetty, aware of the trust fund proposal, hated the idea. She wanted absolute control over the entire fortune.

She tried instead to persuade her aunt that she would be more than capable of handling the fortune after Sylvia's death and should therefore inherit the money free of any constraint. Sylvia for her part resisted this suggestion, not only because of the worsening relationship between her niece and herself, but also because she had genuine concerns about Hetty's financial skills and maturity. The battle between the two of them on this point was waged over several months. Finally, as Sylvia's health continued to worsen, she appeared suddenly to give way to Hetty's wishes. In January 1862, a will under which Hetty was named as principal beneficiary of all of Sylvia's estate (without making use of a trust) was drawn up and signed and witnessed. Hetty appeared to have achieved all that she wished, and she returned to her father in New York as content a young woman as it was probably possible for her to be.

Such contentment was short-lived. It occurred to Hetty on her return to New York that there was nothing at all to prevent Sylvia from preparing and signing a new will, which would invalidate the one just executed and which might not provide for the disposal of Sylvia's estate on the terms Hetty believed had been agreed. And indeed, her concerns grew as Sylvia's health continued to deteriorate, and her need for medical assistance increased, to the extent in fact that Sylvia's physician, Doctor William Gordon actually moved into the house at Round Hill, leaving his wife and children at home. Before long, Sylvia was depending upon him for almost everything, and his influence over her grew rapidly and to Hetty's eyes, in a sinister fashion. He began to prescribe drugs such as laudanum for his patient, and on his instructions, Hetty was advised that in order to keep Sylvia calm, she should no longer visit her aunt.

Hetty was reduced to receiving such snippets of information as she could glean by way of gossip from Sylvia's New Bedford neighbours, and from members of her aunt's staff, especially her aunt's nurse, a woman named Electa Montague, whom Hetty appears to have considered something of a confidant. This was exactly the state of affairs that Hetty had dreaded, with her aunt out of her sight and under the effective control of people who might influence her to Hetty's disadvantage, but she could do very little about it, even when she heard rumours that her aunt had drawn up a new will without telling her. Her father reported to Thomas Mandell, still functioning as the trustee of a portion of the original Howland fortune, that Hetty was "made sick" at the thought, and (apparently without telling Hetty) he asked Mandell, who was involved in at least some of Sylvia's financial affairs, whether Mandell could, without betraying confidences, let him know if there was any truth in the rumours of a new will. Mandell responded with a soothing reply to the effect that Sylvia would make sure that Hetty would be left all the property she would ever need. It is not clear whether this answer was ever passed on to Hetty but in any case, she continued to worry.

In the meantime, the American Civil War, having erupted in April 1861, continued its bloody course, but whilst it brought suffering and anguish to millions, it also created a spectacular economic boom in the northern states for those able to benefit from it. In order to pay for the war, the federal government borrowed and taxed heavily,[9] at least by the

---

[9] It has been estimated by some commentators that prior to 1863, less than 15 percent of the federal government's expenditures were met out of taxation. The expansion of the US tax system during the war, including the introduction of the first form of income tax in American history, meant that by the war's end approximately 25 percent of federal government revenues were met from taxation. As for the balance, alternative sources of finance were identified and developed, including the creation (in 1862) of currency notes which were not backed by gold (so-called "greenbacks") and the simple expedience of

standards of the day, and the financial, commercial and industrial hubs of the northern states such as Boston, Pittsburgh and above all, New York, experienced bursts of intense activity such as they had never experienced before.

Hetty's father was one of those who prospered. His share of the business of William T. Coleman and Company by itself was sufficient to provide him with a large and steadily rising income, in addition to which he made further money by investing in government bonds, stocks and various real estate ventures across the country. He was gaining a reputation, though, of becoming increasingly careful – even miserly - with his money, ever more anxious to see his fortune grow. Even his partner William Coleman with whom Edward enjoyed a cordial business relationship later admitted that Edward Robinson exceeded any man he knew "in ingenious expedients for saving a dollar". It was almost as if Edward realised that he only had a finite amount of time within which to build his fortune, and that time was growing shorter.

If he did have such a presentiment, it was well-founded, for in the spring of 1865, he was suddenly taken ill with a mysterious illness, one which sapped his strength over a number of months. Before long he was largely confined first to his New York home, a brownstone mansion on West 26th Street, and eventually to his bed. During this time, Hetty did her best to care for him, not only acting effectively as his nurse but also assisting him manage his financial interests. Edward for his part seems to have known that he was slowly dying, and worried about two things

---

borrowing money from the public, both at home and overseas. It has been calculated that between 1861 and 1865 the federal debt increased from $65 million to $2.7 billion ($42 billion in today's terms). It was the injection of these new influxes of money into the economy of the northern states that created the economic boom of the war years and played an important part in the development of the United States over the following decades as an industrial superpower.

in particular: first, Hetty's continuing spinster status (she was now aged over thirty, old at that time for a woman to yet be unmarried), and secondly, whether as a woman, and not withstanding her undoubted financial skill and judgment, she would be able to shoulder alone the responsibilities of managing a fortune when the time came for it to pass to her. The answer to both these problems, at least to his eyes, would be for Hetty to marry, and fortunately, he had a potential candidate for Hetty's hand in mind.

Edward Henry Green had been born in Bellows Falls, Vermont in 1821. The son of a reasonably prosperous local businessman, he moved to Boston at the age of seventeen, another one of those young men of the time so eager to move to one of the big east coast cities in search of financial opportunities. After spending nine years in Boston learning the finer points of mercantile trade, he travelled to the Far East, visiting the newly established British colony of Hong Kong before moving to the Philippines where he was to remain for nearly eighteen years. Employed by Russell, Sturgis and Company, a trading firm which had business dealing with William T. Coleman and Company, his trading prowess led him to becoming a millionaire by the age of 44, at which time, still a bachelor, he decided to return home permanently to the United States, and specifically to New York, where his fortune and respectable family background ensured his ready acceptance into the social ranks of the well-to-do.

Whether he was already acquainted with Edward Robinson through business dealings prior to his return is not known, but even if they had not previously met, they must have done so shortly after Edward Green arrived in New York. Nor is it known when Green first met Hetty - there are tales of them having met in Boston as early as 1864, though this seems unlikely, and, it is more probable that they were introduced by Edward Robinson sometime in February 1865 just before the onset of his fatal illness. In any event, it seems that Green and Hetty were much taken with one another, and Edward Robinson, as he began to succumb to his sickness, approved. To his eyes, Green had already proven himself to be a mature and capable businessman, one who had accumulated a significant amount of wealth in his own right and who would, if and when required, be able to provide Hetty with the help, advice and support Edward Robinson believed she would need to assist her in protecting the fortune that he had made. In expressing these views (as he did to some close acquaintances) Edward Robinson reflected the common male view of the day that by and large sons might be trusted with financial affairs, but daughters could not. In doing so, he failed to take into account the obvious fact that Hetty was by no means a typical female of her day when it came to money matters.

Whether or not Hetty knew of her father's views as regards her financial abilities is not entirely clear, but in any event even if she did, it did not prevent a rapid courtship taking place between herself and Edward Green. To some people they made a surprising couple, for Green in many ways was very different from the determined but financially and socially restrained Hetty. He was a tall man, over six feet in height, with a friendly easy-going manner, careful to be well dressed and he enjoyed good food and drink and the company of other people, and was regularly seen attending theatres, balls and dinner parties. He was also openly kind and generous, supporting his now widowed mother who continued to live in Bellows Falls, and seems to have been generally well liked, which was not necessarily always so in the case of Hetty. In any event, and regardless of what other people may have thought, they clearly saw something special in each other, for by the end of May 1865, with Edward Robinson's blessing, they became engaged.

Two weeks later, Edward Robinson died, leaving a personal fortune of over $5.5 million,[10] most of which was invested in stocks, bonds, loans

---

[10] Approximately $86 million today.

and real estate. Hetty's grief at the death of her father who had taught her so much was very real, and there is no doubt that she relied heavily on the emotional support of Edward Green at this time. That support was especially necessary when the provisions of Edward Robinson's will were read, for they reflected the concerns he had expressed about Hetty's ability to manage the fortune he was leaving her. Given the praise he had (sometimes) showered upon her as regards her financial knowledge, Hetty had not unreasonably expected to inherit all, or at least the bulk of that fortune outright, but the will made in March 1865 showed that Edward Robinson had been entertaining other ideas. True, he left her $1 million absolutely,[11] but aside from a few relatively minor bequests to individuals and a donation of $10,000 to the town of South Kingstown, Rhode Island, where he had been born, for the establishment of an educational institution, the balance of his estate was to be held on trust, managed by independent trustees. The trust would provide Hetty with an income but would not allow her to control the underlying capital. That was to remain invested at the discretion of the trustees and would only be distributed when she died, the bulk of it to beneficiaries named in her will (or persons otherwise entitled to inherit under intestacy in the (unlikely) event she left no valid will), and the balance to other members of Edward's family.

There seems little doubt that Hetty was temporarily crushed by the terms of her father's will, notwithstanding that the bequest of $1 million alone made her one of the wealthiest women in the country. She saw her father's will as his final judgment of her and her abilities, and grieving his loss as she was and continued to do, she never really forgave him for what she saw as his betrayal of her. It seems also to have coloured her views of other males managing what she continued to consider to be her money, who she treated with increasing contempt

---

[11] $919,000 in cash plus a property in San Francisco called the North Point Dock Warehouse.

as the years passed. Eventually, that contempt or at least a lack of trust as regards male financial acumen would extend to envelop even Edward Green, but for the time being at least, with her confidence in herself temporarily at a low ebb, she relied heavily on him for emotional and moral support, which he gave to her freely.

Aunt Sylvia's Will

Hetty would have considerable need of Edward Green's support over the months that followed. Less than three weeks after the death of Edward Robinson, Hetty received news that Sylvia had taken a turn for the worse and was thought to be dying. She set off at once to be by her aunt's side, but Sylvia died on 2nd July 1865, before Hetty reached New Bedford.[12] For Hetty, not only was there the pain of losing another close relative so soon after the death of her father, but there was also the continuing anguish about the disposition of Sylvia's estate, and the worry that her aunt had rewritten her will since their apparent agreement in January 1862.

Hetty did not have long to wait to learn the worst. Gossip about the likely size and disposition of Sylvia's estate had spread far and wide, and when her will was read only hours after her funeral, not only was Hetty present (reportedly so heavily draped in black crepe that it was hard to recognise her) but also a crowd of Sylvia's servants, doctors and distant relatives, most of whom not only had hopes of themselves personal benefitting from Sylvia's generosity from beyond the grave, but also were eagerly awaiting the likely reaction of Hetty when she discovered the worst. For as the will began to be read, Hetty realised with mounting anger that it was not the one that she had seen being executed in January 1862, but a later one which Sylvia had signed in September 1863, with some amendments by codicil made in November 1864. It revoked the earlier will entirely, and Sylvia had kept its existence secret from Hetty.[13]

---

[12] Isaac Howland Jr.'s second wife Ruth also died in 1865.

[13] The codicil, interestingly, revoked a gift of $100,000 which would otherwise have been made under the terms of the 1863 will to Edward Robinson. Exactly why Sylvia had at first been minded to give her brother-in-law whom she had

Under the terms of the earlier will, Hetty was to have been left the vast bulk of Sylvia's fortune, now estimated at more than $2 million dollars, not as large an estate as that of Sylvia's old rival, Hetty's father, but large enough. Matters were somewhat different under the provisions of the will of 1863 and the codicil of 1864. There were numerous personal bequests to a number of Sylvia's friends in New Bedford and elsewhere (to several of whom she left individual gifts, mostly $10,000 each, though one widow received $20,000) and gifts to several of her long-suffering servants and personal attendants, with her night nurse, Eliza Brown and Fally Brownell, the housekeeper, each receiving $3,000. Electa received the sum of $5,000. Various trusts of $10,000 were established for other servants. There were, as Sylvia had long hoped, some significant charitable donations, including various bequests to the city of New Bedford, some of which were to be used to improve the city's water supply and a donation of $200,000 to Thomas Mandell. As for Doctor Gordon, Sylvia's svengali-like physician, not only was he named as one of three trustees of the various trusts set up under the will, each of whom could charge reasonable amounts to the estate for carrying out their duties, but he also received $50,000 in cash, as did the other two trustees. Other members of Gordon's family, such as his wife and daughters also benefitted from Sylvia's generosity.

As for Hetty herself, she would only receive $1 million, about half of what she had expected. To make matters worse, half of this was also subject to a trust, so that not only could Hetty only have access to the income it generated, but not the underlying capital, but also one of the trustees in control of this money would be Doctor Gordon, for whom her detestation was growing rapidly. Thomas Mandell would also be

---

disliked for years such a sum is not entirely clear; it may have been an attempt to ensure Edward did not challenge the will. By November 1864, Sylvia seems to have come to the conclusion that any challenge would be unlikely to succeed, and in any event, Edward resolved the question of whether he would challenge by dying before Sylvia.

another of the trustees, and effectively act as the trustees' chairman. Making matters even worse (if that were possible), upon Hetty's death, the capital would pass not simply to her descendants, but would be shared between all the descendants of Gideon Howland Senior, Sylvia's paternal grandfather.

Hetty immediately set about consulting lawyers with a view to overturning the will of 1863 and its codicil. This was easier said than done, for there seemed little doubt that the will and later codicil had been properly drafted, executed and witnessed, and in November 1865, William H Bennett, the judge presiding over the probate court in New Bedford had no difficulties in giving his approval to its execution. However, Hetty claimed she had irrefutable proof that the 1863 will did not reflect the wishes of her aunt, suggesting that improper influence had been brought to bear on Sylvia by those who had most to gain from the later will being upheld as valid, namely Doctor Gordon, members of his family, and the other trustees, and she promptly launched an appeal to the Supreme Judicial Court of Massachusetts. Her alleged proof took the form of a letter dated 11th January 1862 – supposedly an addendum to Sylvia's will of 1862 which Hetty claimed had been attached to Sylvia's copy of that will, and which she had retrieved from Sylvia's bedroom in the presence of Fally Brownell and Electa Montague on the night of Sylvia's funeral, whilst Edward had remained downstairs.[14] The key aspects of the letter read as follows:

> *Be it remembered that I, Sylvia Ann Howland, of New Bedford, in the County of Bristol, do hereby make, publish and declare this the second page of this will and testament made on the eleventh of January in the manner following, to wit: Hereby revoking all wills made by me before or after this one - I give this will to my niece to shew if there appears a will made without notifying her, and without returning her will to her*

---

[14] Hetty claimed she held a second copy of the letter herself.

28

through Thomas Mandell as I have promised to do. I implore the Judge to decide in favor of this will, as nothing would induce me to make a will unfavorable to my niece, but being ill and afraid if any of my caretakers insisted on my making a will to refuse, as they might leave or be angry, and knowing my niece had this will to shew – my niece fearing also after she went away – I hearing but one side, might feel hurt at what they might say of her, as they tried to make trouble by not telling the truth to me, when she was here even herself. I give this will to my niece to shew if absolutely necessary, to have it, to appear against another will found after my death. I wish her to shew this will, made when I am in good health for me, and my old torn will made on the fourth of March, in the year of our Lord one thousand eight hundred and fifty, to show also as proof that it has been my lifetime wish for her to have my property. I therefore give my property to my niece as freely as my father gave it to me. I have promised him once, and my sister a number of times, to give it all to her, all excepting about one hundred thousand dollars in presents to my friends and relations.

In witness whereof I have set thereto my hand and seal this eleventh of January in the year of our Lord one thousand eight hundred and sixty two.

Sylvia Ann Howland (SEAL)

Hetty and her lawyers effectively argued that in 1862, she and Sylvia had been on such close terms that they had entered into a contract to execute "mutual wills", and that the letter was proof of improper influence being brought to bear on a dying woman with the intention of causing a breach of that contract, and grounds for invalidating the 1863 will and the subsequent codicil. This was by no means so clear to other, more disinterested observers, and certainly not to Doctor Gordon and his fellow trustees, though they could hardly be described as disinterested themselves. They had sound reasons for challenging the validity of the letter, and indeed the very notion that Sylvia and Hetty had entered into mutual wills, not least due to the fact that it simply was not legally possible for Sylvia in 1862 to revoke any will that she might subsequently make. Moreover, there was not lacking evidence that Hetty and Sylvia had not always been as close as Hetty now wished to claim. Then too, the wording of the letter was clumsy and it was obvious that no lawyer had drafted it. That of itself would not necessarily have proven fatal to Hetty's argument; there was and is no legal requirement for a will or codicil to be drafted by a lawyer. But given that Sylvia had regularly used the services of her lawyer in her financial affairs, it was surprising to say the least that she had apparently not sought legal advice in relation to the letter, particularly given its potentially contentious nature. Even more problematic for Hetty however was the fact that Sylvia's signature on the letter had only one witness, Hetty herself, and she was most certainly a beneficiary to Sylvia's estate. For all these reasons, the trustees' lawyers had good grounds for being quietly confident that the letter would be set aside and declared to have no effect. Hetty, stubbornly, continued to insist on its validity.

The appeal in the case of *Robinson v Mandell* was heard in December 1865, and it was immediately clear that a great deal of time would be spent investigating the legitimacy, or otherwise, of the letter. In many ways, the appeal was a public relations disaster for Hetty, with the lawyers acting for the trustees calling witness after witness to support their contentions that not only was Hetty a woman of unprepossessing personal habits (her standards of personal hygiene were called into question for instance), and that towards the end of her life, Sylvia had been anxious to keep her at a distance, but also that she was a greedy, unscrupulous, scheming financial opportunist, and a woman who certainly would be more than capable of indulging in a little forgery if she felt it to be necessary. The lawyers had good reason for wanting to make this insinuation, for there was one more aspect of the letter which called its legitimacy into question, namely Sylvia's supposed signatures at the bottom of both the letter Hetty said she had retrieved from Sylvia's bedroom, and the copy of the letter she claimed her aunt had given to her for safekeeping. Even to an untrained eye, the signatures on the two letters looked suspiciously identical not only to each other, but crucially to Sylvia's signature which had adorned her will of 1862. There was no doubt as to the validity of that signature for it had been witnessed by three independent people. Two questions naturally and promptly arose – were the signatures on the two copies of the letter forgeries, and if so, had they been forged by Hetty herself?

This was a serious allegation for the trustees' lawyers to make, for if true, it would potentially expose Hetty to criminal charges, and as the hearings proceeded, she increasingly found herself forced on the defensive. In an attempt to rebut the suggestion of forgery, Hetty's lawyers called expert witnesses, including noted Harvard naturalist Louis Agassiz,[15] and Harvard lawyer and doctor Oliver Wendell Holmes, both of whom examined the later signatures and declared they could see no evidence that they had been produced by tracing the earlier signature on the 1862 will. Other experts called on Hetty's behalf expressed similar opinions, and considerable attention was also paid in attempting to prove that a person might sign his or her signature in nearly identical fashion time after time.

Unfortunately for Hetty, the trustees' lawyers were also capable of calling expert witnesses who reached diametrically opposite conclusions. These included Harvard astronomer and mathematician Benjamin Peirce and his son Charles Sanders Peirce,[16] also a mathematician, who applied statistical analysis to the three signatures,

---

[15] Called because of his skills in using magnifying glasses and microscopes.
[16] Probably best known now as the founder of the Pragmatist school of philosophy and as a logician.

and concluded that the likelihood of a person producing three signatures in such an identical fashion was "once in 2,666 millions of millions of millions of times". The strong implication was that the later signatures were forgeries. As for the declarations by Agassiz and Holmes that they had been unable to identify any evidence of the tracing of the signature on the 1862 will, the impact of their testimonies was significantly muted by an expert demonstrating that signatures could be copied without the use of tracing at all.

Given the sheer volume of testamentary evidence produced in the case, it is unsurprising that once the last expert had presented his views, the judge presiding over the case, Justice Nathan Clifford, was in no hurry to hand down his decision. Whilst the case had been progressing, Hetty, often in the company of Edward Green, had commuted regularly back and forth between Massachusetts and New York. During this period, she had continued to rely heavily on Edward's support, particularly during those trying times when the validity of the signatures was being attacked in the courtroom or in the columns of the various newspapers which were following the progress of the case with avid attention. Now, whilst the judge was deliberating his decision, Edward and Hetty settled in New York. Much of Hetty's attention continued to be focussed on the case, but she and Edward also spent time together reorganising her now substantial investment portfolio. At the same time, Edward pursued his own investment interests, and both he and Hetty were eager to seek new investment opportunities in the economic confusion that followed the end of the Civil War.

The couple also decided the time had come for them to be married, more than two years after they had first become engaged. The necessary arrangements were duly made and their marriage took place on 11th July 1867 in a quiet ceremony held at the New York home of Henry and

Sarah Grinnell. Hetty's maid of honour was Annie Leary,[17] the daughter of a Manhattan hat manufacturer who had made his fortune selling hats to varied members of New York's elite, including the Astors. Hetty had first met Annie during her earlier stay with the Grinnells, and they had remained in touch. The two of them would remain friends for the rest of their lives, disproving the frequently repeated assertion that Hetty had no friends.

In the meantime, rumours continued to abound about the possibility that the court might find that the signatures had been forged, and a criminal investigation launched to discover the likely forger. Hetty was the most obvious suspect (though there had also been some whispered suggestions that Edward might also have been involved, for he had publicly supported Hetty's version of events), and if fingers were not yet being explicitly pointed at Hetty, some were certainly beginning to move in that direction. It may have quietly occurred to Hetty and Edward that whilst they awaited the verdict of the judge, keeping a distance between themselves and potential accusers might have some attractions, and that a honeymoon overseas (conveniently outside the jurisdiction of the United States) might not be a bad idea. Hetty of course was publicly scornful that there was any possibility other than the court ruling in her favour, finding the letters to be genuine and declaring the 1863 will and its codicil to be invalid. Nevertheless, in October 1867 Mrs and Mrs Green boarded the steamship *Russia*, the latest addition to the trans-Atlantic fleet operated by the Cunard line, and set sail for England.

Upon their arrival, Hetty and Edward made their way to London, where probably at Edward's urging, and almost certainly at his expense, they took rooms in the Langham Hotel, which had opened its doors to guests in 1865, with the Prince of Wales cutting the ribbon at

---

[17] She later became Countess Annie Leary, having been granted a papal title for her various acts of philanthropy.

the opening ceremony. The Langham had swiftly established a reputation for sophisticated and expensive luxury, and was proving particularly popular with wealthy American visitors. Edward, who had maintained his links with the firm of Russell, Sturgis and Company whilst in New York, quickly made his presence felt in the City of London, where he effectively became that firm's London agent, with a particular focus on the sale of American railroad bonds to British and European investors. He also served on the boards of several London banks, and generally enjoyed the life of a wealthy gentleman in London. Hetty for her part played the tourist for the first few weeks following their arrival. Around the end of November 1867, she became pregnant, but this did not prevent her from attending to the needs of her own fortune. This involved placing orders for the purchase of US Treasury and state bonds and reinvesting the dividends, as well as investing in various industrial bonds and stocks, especially (no doubt in part thanks to Edward's expertise in the field) those issued by railroad companies. She also continued to buy up US greenback notes, a practice which she had begun in 1865, when she inherited her first significant sum of money from her father.

Greenback notes had fulfilled their initial purpose of helping to fund the North's war effort, but following the end of the Civil War, they had come to be regarded with suspicion by many investors who, deciding they preferred the certainty of gold or silver, had hurriedly sold their holdings of greenbacks, causing their price to fall sharply so that by the end of August 1865, in order to buy $100 worth of gold from the gold market in New York, you needed $144.25 worth of greenbacks. For Hetty, who like a few other astute investors was convinced that the value of greenback notes would eventually recover, this was a marvellous opportunity, even though buying greenbacks went against much of the perceived financial wisdom of the time. Her continuing purchase of greenbacks in the years that followed 1865 probably represents the first clear example on her part of contrarian investing, and time proved the wisdom of her approach. Changes in US government policy, and the passage of various pieces of legislation, such as the Specie Payment Resumption Act of 1875 which effectively if not officially restored the United States to the gold standard on 1st January 1879,[18] caused greenbacks in time to recover their value. When that happened, investors such as Hetty who had bought when the price was low and held on to their greenbacks found they had made significant profits.

There is no doubt that Hetty prospered during her time in London. She later told a friend that the most she made in one day, admittedly not just from the purchase of greenbacks, was $200,000. From her bond investments alone, during her first year in London, she is estimated to have made a profit of $1.25 million. This profit, together with other income which she received, especially from the trust fund established by her father and of which she was a beneficiary (whether she liked it or not) she reinvested, and her fortune continued to grow.

So did her family. On 22nd August 1868, in her rooms at the Langham, she gave birth to a son, whom she and Edward named Edward Howland Robinson Green. He would become known as Ned to his family and close friends, and seemed a healthy child.

The pleasure that Edward and Hetty felt with the arrival of Ned was abruptly shattered on 14th November 1868 when Judge Clifford announced his decision in the case of *Robinson v Mandell*. Few disinterested observers were surprised when Clifford effectively found in favour of the trustees, but what was more surprising was that he did

---

[18] In an attempt to maintain its reserves of bullion during the Civil War, the United States had at least temporarily abandoned the gold standard in 1861. Strictly speaking, the United States did not legally return to the gold standard until 1900, but between 1879 and 1900, the United States maintained a strict policy of inter-convertibility between greenbacks and gold at par value.

so in terms that left Hetty with very little hope of a successful appeal. In nineteen pages of detailed reasoning, he essentially dismissed all of Hetty's evidence in support of her contention that she and Aunt Sylvia had prepared mutual wills, citing a Massachusetts' law limiting the ability of one party to a mutual will to testify on his or her own behalf unless the other party was also alive and able to give testimony. Moreover, it was clear that even if he had been willing to accept Hetty's testimony, he was by no means persuaded that Hetty's will of 1860 and Sylvia's of 1862 together constituted mutual wills, for not only were they signed at different times, but in addition Hetty's will did not cite Sylvia as a potential beneficiary. By adopting this approach, the judge was effectively ruling that Hetty had no viable evidence of any kind to support her arguments, and her claims were dismissed. As regards the question of whether or not the signatures on the letters upon which Hetty had relied so much were forged, the issue that had most intrigued members of the public watching the progress of the case, the judge felt no need to express an opinion,[19] for regardless of how that question was answered, it would not affect the conclusions of the ruling. The frequently tedious days sat hearing the myriad of expert opinions as to whether or not a forgery had occurred were not completely a waste of time however, for the judge did note that the case might in due course prove valuable in helping to establish rules of evidence in future forgery cases, and indeed this later proved to be so.

Hetty's lawyers promptly filed court papers giving notice of her intention to appeal to the United States Supreme Court, though it is by no means clear on what grounds she would have been able to build an appeal. Perhaps luckily for Hetty, there was no need to do so, for she and the trustees were able to reach a compromise a few weeks later, under which she agreed that each beneficiary under Sylvia's will of 1863 should receive the benefit of their various bequests, plus 6 per cent

---

[19] Perhaps for Hetty, that was just as well.

interest annually from the date of Sylvia's death by way of compensation for the late payments of the bequests due to the court proceedings. In return, Hetty would commence to receive the income payments due to her under the trust. When Hetty died, the remaining capital held on trust under the terms of the 1863 will would then be distributed to the heirs of Gideon Howland Senior, as Sylvia had intended. This settlement was essentially a public admission of surrender on Hetty's part, and vindication for the trustees (and for Sylvia); however, just when it looked like matters might finally be settled, another problem arose, which delayed matters once again. This time the question was how taxes due on the bequests should be paid; specifically, should they be met out of the bequests themselves or out of the remaining capital held on trust and intended to generate an income for Hetty? If the latter were to occur, this would reduce the payments Hetty herself would receive. Hetty, unsurprisingly, preferred the first option, but others did not, and the question was referred to the court for a decision. Eventually, one year later, the court held that the taxes should be paid from the capital, and Hetty had to accept she had suffered another defeat.

Once the legal challenges had died away, Sylvia's estate could be distributed. After satisfying the other bequests, it was found that the portion to be held on trust for Hetty had grown in value to about $1.3 million (approximately $24.5 million in today's terms), a sum which was capable of generating an annual income of approximately $65,000. She also received the benefit of a lump sum payment of approximately $600,000 representing interest and dividends which had been accruing on her behalf under the terms of the 1863 will since Sylvia's death and which the trustees had held back from distributing pending the settlement of Hetty's challenge and the tax question. Her share of Sylvia's estate may have been smaller than she had hoped, and she would for the rest of her life chafe about "her money" being under the control of the trustees appointed by Sylvia, but this new money nevertheless improved Hetty's financial strength considerably. She naturally set about investing these new funds with the same degree of assiduity as she paid to her other investments, and her fortune continued to grow. Some of that fortune she now began to apply methodically in a manner for which she would become famous, at least within investing circles, namely by buying mortgages and other loans from banks which had previously been issued to purchasers of land, particularly in the United States. While the borrowers were able to meet their interest and capital repayment obligations, Hetty had yet another, growing source of income which could be applied for investment purposes. If a borrower defaulted (as happened frequently whenever the economy experienced a downturn), she would foreclose and take the property for herself, and in this way over time she began to accumulate significant holdings of real estate.

She also acquired another child, for on 7th January 1871 she gave birth to her daughter, who was christened Harriet Sylvia Ann Howland Green, though within the family she became known as Sylvie. Hetty would claim that naming her daughter after her late aunt was proof of the closeness which during the court case she had insisted existed between Sylvia and herself. She was also known on occasion to cite her daughter's name as evidence that she could not possibly have forged her aunt's signature, though to many of those who heard this declaration, it hardly constituted conclusive proof of Hetty's innocence.

Sylvie's arrival in the world also led Edward and Hetty to decide that after having rented rooms in the Langham Hotel for more than three years, it was time for them to establish a London home of their own, and they and their children, together with a young maid moved to a house on Charlotte Street, Fitzrovia. Near to Bloomsbury and the British Museum, Charlotte Street was respectable, though perhaps lacking the social grandeur of other, more elite (and expensive) areas of the city such as Mayfair or Kensington. It was however less than half a mile away from the Langham Hotel, and thus in a part of London that the Greens by now knew well, and where they felt at home.

The Panic of 1873

For more than two years, Hetty and Edward maintained the life of rich Americans enjoying the pleasures that London had to offer, and indeed those of Europe, for Edward's job would sometimes take him on trips to France, Holland and Germany, and Hetty would on occasions accompany him. Between caring for her children (for, although she made use of nannies and other domestic servants to assist her with childcare, Hetty did spend time with her children, certainly at least as much as many other wealthy mothers of that time and place did), and as ever keeping an eye on her fortune, these were busy years for Hetty. Edward too continued to work hard in the gentleman banker role that he had assumed for himself, though he was still more inclined than Hetty to the casual enjoyments that London at the height of the Victorian era could offer wealthy men, such as membership of clubs, visits to the theatre and sporting events, and invitations to fashionable dinner parties.

The Greens might have stayed in London indefinitely, but in the early 1870s, the economic climate on both sides of the Atlantic began to worsen. Banks and other financial institutions became more cautious about lending money, and the Bank of England raised its interest rates for inter-bank lending, all of which led to a constriction of the money supply. This not only served to put the brake on US financial expansion but also triggered a series of bankruptcies across the country. To make matters worse, a series of scandals involving financial corruption, particularly in relation to the operation of various American railroad companies damaged public confidence not only in the stock market but also in city and state political institutions as well as the federal government itself. Then on 8th September 1873, the New York Warehouse and Securities Company, a major source of funds for railroad companies was forced to close its doors. This was followed on 13th September by the insolvency of infamous New York financier Daniel Drew's firm of Kenyon, Cox and Company. On 18th September, Northern Pacific Railroad announced it could no longer pay its bondholders; this in turn led directly to the collapse of Jay Cooke & Company, one of the most prestigious financial firms on Wall Street. With the collapse of Jay Cooke & Company, panic selling engulfed Wall Street, the beginning of the Panic of 1873. More banks began to fail, two on the same day as Jay Cooke & Company, and no less than 37 on the day after. Stock prices, even those of companies known to be profitable and well managed, fell sharply within a few hours of trading. When the news of the Panic reached London, the stock market there also began to tumble, followed very shortly thereafter by the markets in Europe. Such was the degree of panic and chaos and the financial losses incurred that at 11 am on 20th September, the New York Stock Exchange closed its doors to business for the first time in history. They would remain closed for ten days as financiers and brokers and others tried desperately to coordinate some sort of response to the crisis, but such was the scale and suddenness of the disaster that no effective steps could be taken to address it. Making matters worse, the federal government itself, under the Presidency of Ulysses S Grant seemed unable or unwilling to provide any sort of leadership or guidance, other than platitudes, and some token purchases of federal bonds. In particular, it took no real action to enhance the money supply, which was now severely restricted. The result was the onset of the Depression of 1873, also known as the Long Depression, which would last for at least four years, during which time tens of thousands of businesses would fail and unemployment would soar.[20] Its onset also led the Greens to conclude it was time to return to the United States.

---

[20] It is rather difficult to say how long the Depression of 1873 actually lasted; technically speaking, the Panic of 1873 was followed by 65 months of economic

Edward and Hetty Green, together with their two children, again boarded the liner *Russia* in October 1873 for their return passage to the United States. On their arrival in New York, they stayed briefly in the city, where they met with their various brokers, for Hetty in particular was eager to take advantage of the fall in stock prices which had resulted from the Panic. Then, the Greens made their way to Bellows Falls, Vermont, Edward's hometown, for they had arranged to stay with Anna Green, Edward's mother, who was now living in the house that her son had bought for her. Edward had left the town 35 or so years earlier to seek his fortune; now he was returning not only with his own fortune, but also with a wife who was a millionairess in her own right. Bellows Falls was not a large township, but Hetty's fame as a wealthy woman preceded her, and there was much speculation by the townsfolk as to what Hetty would be like, with some at least expecting some princess-like apparition gliding elegantly through life aided by apparently unlimited reserves of cash which not only would enable her to lay claim to a leading place in what passed for the town's upper social circles but would also no doubt be dispensed liberally in the town's various shops and other businesses. What they saw, and experienced, when Hetty arrived, was very different. Hetty, now in her early forties, had continued the frugal habits of her youth, and had very little interest in dressing in the latest fashions, preferring simple and cheap, even dowdy dresses. She had even less interest in attending sophisticated teas and other social amusements, and generally avoided them. Elegant she was not, and there were those who swore that neither

---

contraction, but other than in 1874, the country's production and GDP continued to grow. Nevertheless, the Panic affected public confidence, and many people felt significantly poorer than they had before its onset. A significant number of business failed following the stock market crash, with more than 18,000 US businesses, including 89 railroads, suffering bankruptcy between 1873 and 1875 alone. More than three million people lost their jobs in the first year of the Long Depression.

Hetty nor her clothes were as clean as they might be (a complaint that had been made about her before and would continue to be made throughout her life). Her manners were abrupt and crude on occasions, and it soon became well known that she was capable of swearing like a trooper when she felt the occasion demanded it.

As for dispensing money liberally, that too the townsfolk soon found was not one of Hetty's notable characteristics. Shortly after her arrival, she decided that her mother-in-law's maid who hitherto had largely been responsible for purchasing food for the household was too profligate (love was not lost between Hetty and Mary, her mother-in-law's maid), and Hetty took it upon herself to make most of the household purchases herself. In practice, this meant she usually returned with the cheapest cuts of meat and the cheapest sacks of groceries she could find, and which she usually only bought after extensive haggling with the local shopkeepers. She became famed in the town for buying only broken biscuits (they were cheaper), and inevitably whenever she passed the local butchers, she would ask them for free scraps of bone and meat for her dog, and would usually be given some. Unsurprisingly, she soon acquired a local reputation not just as someone who was frugal, but as a mean penny-pinching miser. Along with the accusation of uncleanliness, this reputation too would follow her for the rest of her life.

Edward and his mother inevitably became tainted by Hetty's fast diminishing reputation. Anna at least did not have to suffer Hetty too long, for she died on 28th June 1875. She was seventy three, and may have suffered from declining health for some time. This did not prevent Mary, still a member of the household despite having threatened to quit on several occasions due to Hetty's overbearing manners, from claiming that Anna's treatment at the hands of her daughter-in-law had hastened her end. As for Edward, he began to resent the jokes and innuendoes he increasingly had to bear thanks to Hetty, and began to realise that

Hetty's values, habits and outlook on life were very different from his own. Their relationship strained, but for the moment, though Edward seethed quietly about Hetty's behaviour, open disagreement between them or protest on his part was relatively rare and muted.[21] One exception to this came shortly after the death of his mother, when they sat down to dinner and Edward discovered Hetty had ordered that only old and cheap glassware should be laid on the table, instead of the valuable crystal glassware his mother had been accustomed to use. When questioned about it, Hetty had simply commented that she had ordered the crystal glassware to be packed away; there was no point in risking damage to valuable glasses when cheap ones would do just as well. According to Mary, Edward had just looked at Hetty with mounting anger, flung a glass against the wall so it shattered, and walked out of the room.

Despite rising tensions between them, they continued to live as man and wife for the next few years. During this time, Edward's ability to fight his corner with Hetty was limited by the fact that his own fortune was taking a battering thanks to the Long Depression. From time to time, he would attempt to replenish his bank accounts by entering into ever more risky investment ventures, usually against Hetty's advice. When he suffered losses, which he frequently (but not always) did, she would usually step in to rescue him. Having to be rescued by his wife did nothing to assuage Edward's increasing irritation with Hetty; for her part, Hetty was increasingly of the view that Edward, like so many other people, was irresponsible with money, and was determined to keep her affairs separate from his.

---

[21] When it became time for Mary to depart, which she did shortly after Anna's death, Hetty refused to pay her the last pay check which she was owed. Mary marched up to Edward in front of several friends and shamed him into settling her wages as his friends watched on, which also did not help relations between Hetty and Edward.

In the meantime, though, Hetty and Edward and their children moved into a large house known as Tucker House which Edward bought in 1875. For the time being it became their family home, though there were frequent trips to New York so that Edward could hold business meetings with colleagues (frequently at his club) and Hetty could consult with and instruct her bankers and brokers, generally at their offices. By now, she was primarily using the services of John J. Cisco, a conservative investment banker who had previously acted for her father, and who had offered his services when she first returned to New York in 1873. Edward used Cisco's banking services as well, but Hetty emphasised to Cisco that her wealth deposited with Cisco was not to be used in any of Edward's ventures.

It was possibly during one of these trips that her son Ned suffered an accident which would lead to one of the most enduring stories that is told about Hetty, one that is almost certainly largely inaccurate so far as Hetty's actions are concerned. According to most versions of the story, Ned had been playing in a park after a heavy snowstorm. He had been given a sled by Edward and Hetty, but was not skilled in its use and managed to injure his knee whilst trying to ride it.[22] The accident may have dislocated his knee cap; in any event Ned continued to walk on it once the pain had disappeared and for a time all seemed well. Later though, possibly several years later, back in Bellows Falls, Ned fell from a tree and injured the leg again, and this time the injury was worse. A doctor was sent for but was delayed, so Hetty washed and bandaged the wound herself, applying a poultice. By her own admission, when the doctor finally arrived, Hetty dismissed him without allowing him to see Ned, who seemed to be recovering, claiming that if the doctor

---

[22] There is some uncertainty as to when the accident happened. Some commentators believe that it happened in New York during the winter of 1873/74, before the move to Bellows Falls, whilst others claim it happened in Bellows Falls a year or so later.

examined the boy, he would expect to be paid, even if there was nothing he could do. From this seems to have sprung the idea that Hetty refused to pay for Ned to receive medical treatment for his injury.

Unfortunately, Ned's leg refused to heal properly; Hetty tried various home remedies, including the application of tobacco leaves to the wound, in an attempt to cure her son (exactly where Edward was whilst all this was going on, and what he thought of his son's treatment in this case is unclear) but to no avail, and Ned's leg continued to cause him severe pain and indeed, began to shrivel and grow malformed, presumably due to a lack of proper use as he grew. Hetty was never keen on consulting doctors it must be said (she had a low opinion of the skills of many of them, and she might well have been right to be cautious given the relatively basic level of medical knowledge of most doctors at that time); nevertheless, she did eventually consult several doctors about Ned's leg, and they all declared that the leg must be amputated. Hetty refused to even consider this option, and the search for a cure for Ned continued.

Hetty Declares Independence

In March 1884, John J. Cisco died, and control of his firm of Cisco & Son passed to his son John A. Cisco and his financial partner Frederick Foote. Hetty regarded this change with some caution, for whilst she had in time come to approve of John J. Cisco's conservatism in financial matters, she was less convinced that this was a trait shared by his son or by Foote. Nevertheless, she continued to use the firm's services, and to keep a considerable sum on deposit there, continually stressing that her money was not to be used for ventures without her express and prior permission. Her suspicions with regard to John A. Cisco and Foote were not misplaced; they were heavily involved in speculation in various railroads, both on their own behalf and on behalf of the firm, and Edward Green had joined them in some of their financial ventures. In Edward's case, this was yet another attempt to stabilise and revitalise his finances, which had continued generally to worsen despite the occasional burst of prosperity.

In May 1884, financial irregularities in the books of the Louisville and Nashville Railroad Company, a railroad company which previously had been generally considered to be safe, respectable and profitable, became public knowledge. The result was a sharp decline in the price of its stock, and considerable panic on Wall Street, for many Wall Street investors had invested in the company's shares, including Cisco, Foote, and Edward. Edward also served on the board of directors of the Louisville and Nashville, though apparently without knowledge of the financial irregularities. Like many other investors, Edward had bought his shares on margin, borrowing the money to do so from Cisco & Son; now that firm pressed Edward for more money to support his margin accounts, threatening to seize and sell his shares if he failed to pay. Edward was so financially overstretched that, to Hetty's fury, he was forced to hand over the deeds for the Tucker House to Cisco & Son. Exactly what happened after that is not entirely clear, but it seems that Hetty was again forced to step in to help her husband out from the financial hole into which he had fallen. Presumably she did so by making funds available to the firm, because in June 1884, the firm transferred the deeds for the Tucker House to Hetty alone.

In the meantime, the troubles of Cisco, Foote and Edward, and those of Cisco & Son itself were not over. At some point in 1884, they had all invested in large quantities of bonds issued by the Houston and Texas Central Railroad, a company which had subsequently fallen under the control of a group of investors headed by railroad magnate Collis Potter Huntington. Huntington and his colleagues were known to be interested in building a new trans-continental railroad system in the south of the country which would effectively mirror much of the Central Pacific route which had been constructed in the 1860s,[23] and it was anticipated that the Houston and Texas Central would form part of the southern route, generating huge profits for the company, and its bondholders. Unfortunately, after he acquired the company, Huntington announced that the finances of the Houston and Texas Central were far worse than he had realised, and that the bond interest payments due on 1st January 1885 would not be honoured. The value of the bonds dropped sharply as a result, losing almost 50 per cent of their value within a few weeks. Not only was this catastrophic for the personal finances of Cisco, Foote and Edward, it was also dire from the perspective of Cisco & Son. Rumours began to spread that the firm was in trouble, and some clients began to withdraw their assets from the bank. It was not an actual run on the bank (at least not yet), but concerned investors and onlookers generally were keeping wary eyes on what might happen next.

---

[23] Huntington had earlier played an important role in the creation of the Central Pacific route.

Hetty now had more than half a million dollars of cash on deposit with Cisco & Son, and the bank was also holding over $26 million worth of her securities in its vaults, making her by far the most important of the firm's customers. When news of the firm's difficulties reached her ears, she immediately wrote a letter demanding that her account be closed at once and her money transferred to the Chemical National Bank of New York.

Hetty was quite within her rights to demand this, but Cisco refused to honour her instructions, pointing out that whilst she might be the bank's largest creditor, her husband owed the firm over $700,000, partly as a result of the losses he had sustained in relation to the Louisville and Nashville and the Houston and Central Texas Railroads, and partly as a result of other failed speculations in which he had indulged using money he had borrowed from the bank. Cisco and Foote now wanted Hetty to settle her husband's debts.

Hetty for her part had always made it clear her money should not be used to underwrite Edward's speculations, and when she learned of the stance taken by Cisco and Foote, she immediately threatened to sue them, and the firm. Knowing Hetty as they did, they must have concluded that she was in deadly earnest, for on 15th January 1885, after the New York Stock Exchange had closed for the day, they announced that Cisco & Son was closing its doors. Hetty on hearing the news immediately set out for New York. On her arrival in the city, she presented herself the doors of the bank, and demanded admittance, expecting to find either Cisco or Foote, either of whom she believed she would be able bend to her will. But control of the bank had already been passed to Lewis May, who had been appointed assignee for the firm (effectively its administrator) and was responsible for ensuring that the dissolution of the firm was carried out in as orderly a fashion as possible, and when Hetty demanded her money, May simply refused to pay, notwithstanding that Hetty was in the right. The same thing happened the next day when she returned once again.

Hetty now had a difficult choice to make. She could have sued as she had threatened to do, but that was a process that might take months, or even years – May himself warned Hetty that the process might easily take a year, that he was not inclined to hurry matters along – and it was open to debate as to whether the firm might last for so long, at least as a solvent entity, which for the time being at least, it probably still was. Then too, Hetty might not win in court – she remembered the legal defeats that she had suffered in relation to Sylvia's will. Furious though she was, she took some time to think matters over and then in early February she agreed grudgingly to pay off Edward's debt to the bank, which by then amounted to a little over $702,000. She gathered up her remaining securities and what remained of her cash, and headed off by cab to the offices of the Chemical National Bank, which welcomed their new customer with open arms.

There is no doubt that Hetty was livid about being forced to underwrite Edward's debts, and she swore she would one day be revenged on the principal architects of her fate, at least as she saw them, namely Cisco, Foote and May, though from that time on she also nursed a bitter hatred for Collis Huntington for reneging on the bond payments which had jeopardised Cisco & Son in the first place. She promised herself that the time would come when she would face them in the courts; for the time being however, she had to content herself with the thought of revenge to come, for she was too busy ensuring that Edward would never again threaten her fortune.[24]

---

[24] Hetty's attempt to take revenge on Lewis May in the courts took place nearly two years later, when she initiated a claim against him in January 1887 before the New York State Supreme Court, just as May was concluding the winding-up of Cisco & Son, and preparing to distribute assets to its creditors. Her case against May effectively consisted of allegations that May had improperly

The closing of Cisco & Son effectively marked the end of Hetty's marriage to Edward though they would remain on civil terms (most of the time) for the rest of their lives. Edward would sometimes be around Hetty one way or another[25] but never again would he be in a position to do more than subsist as best he could on her financial coattails. Never again would he have access to her money – in any way – and never again did Hetty seek his advice. From now on, she would protect herself and her fortune, for the benefit of herself and ultimately her children.

Over the next two decades, Hetty devoted herself almost entirely to business, and the multiplication of her fortune many times over. It was also during these years that the caricature of Hetty as the Witch of Wall Street as we now know it today came into full being. Never one to follow a crowd, during the years that proved to be the apogee of the Gilded Age, whilst many of Hetty's fellow multi-millionaires vied with one another to dazzle the world with their wealth, Hetty deliberately adopted an unostentatious lifestyle, frequently renting drab apartments in boarding houses, where she would stay for a month or two with Ned and Sylvie (when they were not away at school), before moving on elsewhere. During this time, she roamed back and forth primarily between New Bedford, Brooklyn and New Jersey, but she travelled elsewhere as well, especially to Chicago, where she had acquired

---

received commission payments during the course of his administration of the stricken bank, or in other words, that he was a fraudster. These were strong allegations to make against a man who had previously been praised by the same court for the "exemplary" conduct of his handling of the bank's affairs whilst it was being wound-up, and Hetty did not help herself during the conduct of the trial by insisting on questioning May and other witnesses (including John Cisco) herself in such an aggressive manner that she not only raised stern objections from the presiding judge, but also from her own lawyers. Inevitably, she lost, and was obliged to pay the costs of the case, estimated at over $10,000.

[25] Though as time went by, he was increasingly to be found at the Union Club in New York, especially when Hetty and the children were residing at the Tucker House.

significant real estate investments upon which she liked to keep an eye. This real estate largely consisted of commercial properties which had been offered as collateral for monies loaned by Hetty to their former owners, and which Hetty had seized when those borrowers had subsequently been unable to repay their loans.

Private by nature and feeling little or no need to court publicity,[26] Hetty herself claimed from time to time that her adoption of an itinerant style of living was simply a demonstration of sensible frugality, and proof that she was remaining true to her Quaker upbringing, reflecting a quite proper refusal to flaunt her wealth, and there was a lot of truth to this. She was not ashamed to mix with ordinary people, felt no need to boast about her wealth and did not hesitate to use public transport such as streetcars or public railroads, or to eat in local restaurants or to shop in local grocery stores (and when she did, she continued to haggle as well as she had ever done). Her unwillingness to spend money on what she considered unnecessary fripperies, such as fashionable clothing, instead frequently wearing the same old dresses (without feeling too much of a need to have them regularly cleaned or repaired) accentuated her reputation for frugality and eccentricity amongst those who knew and recognised her, but many of those she passed in the street on a daily basis had not the slightest idea that they had just walked by one of the wealthiest people in the country, indeed the world.

There were those though who questioned whether Hetty's itinerant lifestyle was simply the result of strict character and values; by adopting that lifestyle, seldom staying long in any one place, Hetty not only escaped the necessity of maintaining small armies of staff to wait upon her (something her fellow multi-millionaires took for granted), but also

---

[26] Although she objected to being pursued by newspaper reporters - another reason to move around so frequently - Hetty did sometimes grant interviews to newspaper and magazine journalists, many of whom seem to have departed more impressed by her than they had expected.

effectively managed to avoid establishing tax residency in any one location, which in turn meant she was able to avoid becoming liable for assessment to property and other local taxes. As far as is known, Hetty never confirmed that such considerations influenced her choice of lifestyle, but she never denied it either.

In any event, such was the lifestyle she adopted following the collapse of Cisco & Son, and her seizure of financial independence, and she effectively maintained it for the rest of her life. It must be said that she was not completely unapproachable – she did socialise with members of her family and she regularly saw friends such as Annie Leary, who by now was increasingly involved in Catholic philanthropy and well on her way to being made a papal countess. But it was business that occupied most of Hetty's time. She regularly appeared at the offices of the Chemical National Bank on Broadway, simply settling herself at any desk in the Bank's entrance hall that happened to be free, and putting herself to work on the day-to-day management of her money – reading financial reports, newspapers and legal documents which she pulled forth from deep within her pockets or from a worn but capacious handbag which she nearly always carried with her, clipping coupons for her dividends and discussing the affairs of the market with the various Bank staff who hovered around her, anxious to ensure that their most important customer was satisfied and protected from the unwanted attention of others. She investigated investment opportunities avidly, continuing to specialise principally in railroad companies and real estate ventures, but she only committed herself to any particular investment once she was satisfied that she had learned all she could about it and concluded that the investment was worth the risk.

One notable aspect of Hetty's approach to investing was that she very much operated alone, and avoided as far as possible entering into any formal partnerships with others. Even when it appeared that she was operating in concert with others, and on occasions of course, she did, it was rarely clear to outsiders how far her commitment to her fellow investors might extend. The classic example of her approach to working with others that is often cited is her involvement in the affairs of the Georgia Central Railroad, a railroad system based in Savannah and which had been pieced together from a number of smaller railroad companies in the years immediately following the end of the Civil War. By the beginning of the 1880s, it possessed about two thousand miles of track, making it one of the larger railroads in the South which was still recovering from the War, but it also had a history of being poorly managed, and fierce competition from rival companies had led to it suffering significant financial damage. Its shares as quoted on the stock market reflected this; they were typically valued at around $68 to $70, and its reported dividend yields were meagre.

Yet, to far sighted investors, the company had some notable positive attributes, not least the layout of its tracks, which allowed an easy flow of produce from the agricultural heartland of much of the South to the port of Savannah, and its interests in a steamship line operating out of Savannah which promised potential access to the expanding markets of the North. Sometime in early 1886, a group of investors, mostly from New York, determined to acquire the Georgia Central. Using a company known as the Richmond Terminal Railroad, they began to buy Georgia Central stock, hoping to gain control of the company. To do this, they needed to control a majority of the shares, and ideally control needed to be achieved by the end of the year, for the Georgia Central's directors were due to stand for re-election in January 1887.

Before long brokers were busy on behalf of Richmond Terminal buying up all the shares of the Georgia Central that they could lay their hands on. For their part, the directors of the Georgia Central rapidly awoke to the dangers posed by the northern investors. With emotions still raw so soon after the conclusion of the Civil War, Georgia Central's directors did not shrink from calling their rivals northern carpetbaggers, and soon a fierce fight was underway for control of the company.

The investors in control of the Richmond Terminal Railroad were not the only ones who had spotted the potential of the Georgia Central. Hetty had herself been quietly buying up the company's stock, and by the summer of 1886, she owned 6,700 shares, a large enough holding to give her a significant influence on the battle for the company. Whoever could acquire control over Hetty's shares was likely to be able to claim a majority shareholding and gain victory.

By November, demand for shares of the Georgia Central had forced the price of its stock up to $100 per share, and given that Hetty had acquired most of her shares for around $70 a share, she would have made a significant profit had she decided then simply to sell them on the open market. Aware of the battle underway for control of the company, however, she elected to wait and watch, confident that sooner or later one side or another would approach her with an offer. Her wisdom in waiting became apparent a few weeks before Christmas, when she was approached by members of the syndicate controlling the Richmond Terminal, headed by E P Alexander. He was the man intended by the syndicate to be appointed president of the Georgia Central once its takeover had been achieved. Alexander and his colleagues approached Hetty offering to buy her shares for $115 per share. Had she accepted the offer there and then, she would have made a profit of more than $300,000 but, sensing the need of Alexander and his colleagues, she declined the offer flat. Her shares were for sale to anyone, she assured them, for the right price, but that price was considerably in excess of $115. It was in fact $125 per share. This was a brave move by Hetty, for if the Richmond Terminal syndicate had managed to achieve control of the Georgia Central without Hetty's help, its share price might well have slumped back again and Hetty would have been left with a significant but minority shareholding that she may later have found difficult to sell at a profit.

Whether or not Alexander and his fellow investors thought such considerations might cause Hetty to rethink her position is not known, but in any event, Hetty refused to alter her price or position, and the Richmond Terminal syndicate members left without agreeing a deal. A little while later though, they returned in order to make a counter-offer. Hetty could have her price of $125 per share, but only after the board election in January had taken place; until then, Hetty would have to promise to vote her shares as the Richmond Terminal syndicate directed. Hetty responded that if that was the approach the syndicate wished to pursue, the price would be $130, not $125. By this time, if they hadn't before, Alexander and his colleagues surely must have realised the mettle of the woman they were dealing with. Still, there was further negotiation, and eventually it was agreed that Hetty would wait until after the election before being paid for her shares, and until then would vote her shares as Alexander and his colleagues wished. Her price for agreeing to this was $127.50 a share. After the election took place, and Richmond Terminal gained control of the Georgia Central and Alexander assumed the presidency of its board of directors, Hetty sold her shares for a total of $854,250, giving her a profit of more than $385,000.

Training an Heir

Though many of her contemporaries might have expressed other opinions, making money simply for the sake of doing so was not the only driving force which motivated Hetty. Staying true to the family values that had helped to create the original Howland fortune, Hetty was also increasingly keen to ensure that she had a worthy heir who could help her to continue to build her fortune during the time that remained for her in this life, and who would have the necessary skills to assume control of that fortune after her death. The burdens and complexities of that fortune were growing rapidly, and though Hetty would never be willing to fully relinquish control of it or her financial freedom, as she grew older, the need for a reliable assistant also grew. For this task, believing as she did in the importance of keeping financial affairs within the family, there were really only two potential contenders for this role, namely, Sylvie or Ned. In practice there was only one for Hetty.

Despite expressing firm opinions on the desirability of women being trained to understand financial matters and learning how to control and use money, and despite having benefitted herself from the financial teachings of her father and grandfather, she seems to have spent little time seeking to impart her financial skills and knowledge to her daughter. For the time being at least, Sylvie, having failed to shine in any notable way at the rather dismal convent school[27] to which she had been sent in her mid-teens, was destined to remain little more than her mother's dependant and her frequent companion. Sylvie must have been increasingly frustrated by these limitations as she grew to

---

[27] Apparently Annie Leary persuaded Hetty that her children might benefit from Catholic education.

adulthood but seems to have made little or no attempt to break free of the circumscribed life decreed for her by her mother.

In contrast, Hetty made little attempt to hide her favouring of Ned as her successor. As he grew older, she began to try to instil in him some of the financial lessons and experiences she had absorbed since she had been a girl.

Ned too may from time to time have felt frustrated at the power Hetty wielded over his life and destiny, but his was a different position from Sylvie's. First, being male afforded him many more opportunities than his sister enjoyed to explore the world and learn about himself. Also, although he was in the interesting position of being an only son and heir to a fortune held by a family which did not live anything like the lifestyle that could have been afforded, and thus was often denied many of the opportunities of enjoying the fruits of fortune open to the children of other wealthy families, Ned was too smart not to appreciate that the time would come when he would be wealthy in his own right. He was genuinely interested in at least some of the financial lessons Hetty could and did try to teach him, and as he grew older, and especially after he left school (he attended St John's College at Fordham, New York, which later became Fordham University) he became increasingly involved in his mother's various business affairs and interests, albeit usually under her direction and ultimate control.

Before he was given anything like true financial responsibility, he had an ordeal to go through which inevitably affected him for the rest of his life. The leg which he had damaged as a child, and for which Hetty had sought so many different treatments, had stubbornly refused to heal, causing him frequent pain. By the time Ned was in his teens, his limp had become pronounced, causing him to trip frequently, which in turn often led to further damage to his leg. In July 1888, he tripped and fell down some steps at the Union Club in New York. Carried to a private room, he was examined by Dr Charles McBurney, who identified a gangrene infection and pronounced there was no option but to remove the leg. The operation was carried out at the Roosevelt Hospital in New York by McBurney himself, who amputated Ned's leg above the knee. Ned bore the operation stoically and in due course had a cork prosthetic leg fitted which allowed him some degree of mobility, and more importantly permitted him to face the rest of his life without the prospect of his leg growing still worse. Hetty refused to recognise that Ned's operation in any way impeded her plans for him, and his recovery from the operation really marked the beginning of Ned's involvement in Hetty's financial affairs.

He would have to start at the bottom though, for Hetty, although she was certainly protective of her son, had no intention of indulging in nepotism. She wanted to instil a sense of self-reliance in him and he acknowledged in later life that this was the most important lesson Hetty had taught him. Self-reliance for Hetty included the concepts of gaining practical experience in whatever area a person wished to master and learning to apply that experience. These were precepts which Ned in time came to adopt for himself.

Starting at the bottom for Ned meant joining the Connecticut River Railroad Company based in Springfield, Massachusetts as a clerk and handyman. Hetty had been a significant investor in the company for years and a frequent user of its services, and meant for Ned to learn the practical aspects of the railroad business. This included him helping to repair track, clearing weeds and learning how to run a locomotive engine, all of which he did notwithstanding his cork leg.

After several months of this, Hetty must have decided Ned had learned a sufficient amount about the railroad business to allow him to take on new responsibilities and a new assignment, for she sent him to Cincinnati, where he worked for the Ohio and Mississippi Railroad, first as a superintendent and then as managing director.

In 1890, Hetty gave him his first significant assignment when she dispatched him to Chicago with instructions to help manage some of her investments there, including overseeing some mortgages, and collecting payments due on them that had fallen into arrears. He was also instructed to keep his eyes open for fresh investment opportunities. Before he departed, Hetty gave him advice that he would never forget. He should know to the penny how much the mortgages were worth, both as regards the principal sums and the interest payments. If the mortgagor owed money, she told Ned, he should insist on payment being made, and should not agree to "take a penny less. And not a penny more". As regards possible new investments (for Ned was now authorised to enter into new agreements on behalf of his mother, but carefully warned too that he would be held responsible for any decision he took), Hetty told him "If anyone is fool enough to offer you the full amount, take it. If you are offered less, tell the man you will give him the answer in the morning. Think the matter over carefully in the evening. If you decide that it will be to our advantage to accept the offer, say so the next day. In business generally, don't close a bargain until you have reflected upon it overnight."

Hetty was aware that Ned would be called upon to indulge in at least some entertaining of business associates, and though it was something she seldom felt the need to do herself, accepted that in this at least, Ned was different from her, if only because he was more sociable. But even here, she gave him sage advice: "After your business is over, you may take him to dinner, and the theater, or allow him to take you, but wait until the transaction has been closed and the money paid." Good advice for a young man in a strange new city.

Just before his departure for Chicago, Ned was given a further task by Hetty. Handing him a satchel she said was filled with valuable securities, she admonished him to keep it safe at all times and to ensure that he delivered it personally to her agent in Chicago. The thought of what might happen if he lost the satchel, or if the securities were stolen, haunted Ned for the entire journey. Stuffing the satchel beneath the mattress in his Pullman sleeping compartment, he barely slept at all, and was exhausted when his train pulled into Chicago's Union Station. He immediately made his way to the agent's office and passed over the parcel of documents which his mother had placed in the satchel. Watching the agent carefully cut open the parcel, he was astonished when the agent let out a laugh and showed Ned the contents. The parcel contained nothing more than worthless outdated insurance policies. Ned would later tell the story with a laugh, claiming it was another example of the way his mother sought to test his reliability, but one wonders if Ned immediately saw the funny side when he first laid eyes on the contents of the satchel that he had guarded so carefully.

In any event, Ned was now in Chicago, which was to be his home for the next three years. His mother was determined that whilst he was there, he should live frugally, and provided him with a less than generous daily allowance. She did however agree that he should enjoy comfortable accommodation, and it was arranged that he should stay at the Auditorium Hotel, which had been completed only the year before and was considered one of the finest hotels in the country. It had been designed by the famous architects Louis Sullivan and Dankmar Adler as a cultural and financial nexus, so that as well as providing four hundred rooms for visitors, all fitted out to the latest high standards, the hotel was attached to the new Auditorium Theatre, primarily intended for Grand Opera productions. There was also a business complex comprising 136 offices, and the hotel was popular with travelling businessmen as well as those keen to appreciate a little culture. Ned no doubt enjoyed the hotel's luxury, but his room there cost six dollar a night, and Ned may have reasoned that if he could get cheaper rooms elsewhere, he would have more spending money to enjoy for himself. In any event, he soon moved out of the Auditorium Hotel and into the

Clifton Hotel situated on the corner of Monroe Street and Wabash Avenue, a perfectly respectable, even luxurious hotel, but one whose rates were only half those of the Auditorium Hotel. Unfortunately for Ned, he neglected to tell Hetty of this impromptu piece of economising, and when she found out, she promptly wrote to him saying "I notice that you are not staying at the hotel I suggested. It is all right, but I have reduced your daily allowance by $3. You are not to have any more spending money than the amount decided on originally."

The arrival of twenty two year old Ned in Chicago caused quite a commotion in that city's business world, and Ned was soon ensconced most days in an office on the eleventh floor of the Owings Building, an office block owned by his mother,[28] entertaining a train of visitors who were as anxious to make the acquaintance of the only son of one of Chicago's most powerful landlords as he was to meet them. Amongst the visitors were reporters, for Ned rapidly discovered he enjoyed giving interviews to newspapers and magazines, and they in turn were eager for the spicy quotes they soon found he was more than capable of delivering. Before long, Ned was announcing all sorts of grandiose plans to the world, such as the creation of a new private bank. "Arrangements are practically completed for the new business" he promised readers of the New York Times. "Ours will be a mortgage business. We will loan money on securities and nothing more. We will loan at a reasonable rate of interest and borrowers may take up their paper at any time." Ned went on to say that the new bank's business would be conducted on the principle of the Chemical National Bank of New York, and that it would be under the control of his mother and himself. "We never invest in anything unless we have control of it" he declared.

---

[28] And Chicago's first fourteen floor skyscraper which had been completed only a few months before Ned's arrival in the city.

Exactly what Hetty thought of pronouncements such as this, or others such as Ned's declaration that the Green family were thinking of buying a major newspaper, is not clear, for she was usually careful not to criticise Ned in public. In private however, if she felt he had transgressed, she did not hesitate in telling him so. Ned later admitted she was capable of giving him "hell" if she thought the circumstances warranted it. It was soon noticeable that neither the establishment of a private bank nor the acquisition of a newspaper showed any signs of occurring in the near future (and in fact they never did), and Ned began to settle down to do what his mother wanted him to do, that is, to manage and expand the family's financial interests in Chicago.

Ned's arrival in Chicago was opportune, for in November 1890, the near collapse of the famous Baring Brothers bank in London following unwise investments forays in South America led to a short but acute recession not only in Great Britain, but across the world, most especially in South America where the financial damage suffered by countries such as Brazil and Argentina was severe. In the United States, the financial concerns emanating from London were compounded by the Sherman Silver Purchase Act of 1890, which had been enacted on 14th July 1890. This Act, which formed part of the drama then being played out between those who favoured the dollar resting on a strict gold standard, and those who wanted some form of bi-metallic gold and silver standard, required the US Treasury to make monthly purchases of four and a half million ounces of silver. The purchases were to be paid for by a form of Treasury notes which in turn were to redeemable for either gold or silver. The problem was that holders of the notes (particularly those who were overseas) were far more likely to insist on their notes being redeemed by gold rather than silver, and the result was that gold began to drain out of the country. This in turn began to affect both stock prices and the price of real estate, both of which began to fall, and eventually led to the Panic of 1893 and the long years of depression and economic adversity which would follow. This was a disaster for many people, but for those with spare money to invest, it was a wonderful opportunity, and Hetty had money. At Hetty's direction, and sometimes with her standing at his side, for she frequently travelled west to visit her son, Ned busied himself scouting opportunities, paying particular attention to those with mortgaged properties who were now in financial difficulties as a result of the increasingly depressed economy. With cash freely available, Hetty and Ned were able to step in and offer to purchase the mortgages. The original mortgagees (typically, but not always, distressed local banks) were often willing to sell the mortgages they held for a fraction of their face values. This, as we have seen already, was one of Hetty's favourite investment stratagems. A mortgage paid regular income with interest on capital well above bank saving rates, with the property as security. If a mortgagor failed to keep up with the payments, however, Hetty with Ned's assistance would claim the property[29] by way of foreclosure, adding it to her growing portfolio of real estate properties. She was also known to wait until a local bank had foreclosed on a property, and then make an offer to the bank to buy the property from them at a fraction of its value before the recession. Often the bank's own finances were fairly strained, and Hetty's offer would be accepted. In this way, Hetty's real estate empire grew rapidly in the early 1890s in and around Chicago, and in other cities too, including St Louis, New York and Boston.

---

[29] Sometimes the property might be a church. Hetty never allowed spiritual considerations to interfere with business. On at least one occasion later in her life, when she held the mortgage on a church in Chicago which had defaulted on its loan, various pastors associated with the church wrote to her, effectively threatening her with hell-fire if she proceeded with the foreclosure. If they were trying to bully her, it backfired spectacularly. She wrote back noting that if that was the case, they had best climb up into their pulpits and pray for her soul "for I am going to foreclose". And she did.

Ned worked in Chicago for his mother for more than two years. No doubt he learned a great deal about the ways of business, and Hetty seems to have recognised this, for in late 1892, she told him that she needed him to help her with some problems she was encountering with some railroad investments she had been making, and was continuing to make, in Texas. She may also privately have decided it was time to seek her revenge against one of those she held responsible for costing her several hundred thousand dollars during the closure of Cisco & Son, namely Collis P Huntington.

Texas

Collis Potter Huntington was born in the town of Harwinton, Connecticut in 1821. His family had been farmers, but the farming life had not particularly appealed to him, and he had left home at 16 to pursue the travelling life of a peddler. In 1842, in partnership with one of his brothers, he had set up a reasonably successful merchandise retail business in Oneonta in the state of New York, but like many young Americans of his time, the discovery of gold in California in 1848 had a powerful allure for him, and by 1849 he was in Sacramento. At first eager to seek his fortune in the goldfields, it had not taken him long to realise that panning for gold was unlikely to lead to a fortune, and that he would make more money by selling mining equipment and other necessities to other, more optimistic gold-miners than himself. With a partner, Mark Hopkins, he set up a hardware store in Sacramento, and soon was successful, and well on the way to becoming rich.

In 1860, he and Hopkins became involved with two other businessmen, Leyland Stanford and Charles Crocker,[30] in a plan to create a railroad system which would form the western link of America's first transcontinental railroad, a system which became known as the Central Pacific. The success of this project led to Huntington (and his colleagues) becoming powerful and sometimes controversial railroad tycoons, and in the process, very rich. For Huntington, his interest in the Central Pacific had just been the start, and within a few years, he was investing in railroad enterprises across the nation, including the Southern Pacific, a relatively new railroad company originally intended to create rail links between San Francisco and San Diego and which eventually would have railroad lines running from New Orleans

---

[30] In time, they became known as the "Big Four".

through Texas and into California, and the Chesapeake and Ohio Railroad, which provided important transportation links between the coal fields of West Virginia and the expanding industrial plants of Ohio and Illinois. An important part of the Southern Pacific system was played by the Houston and Texas Central, still under Huntington's control, and which had been significant in the demise of Cisco & Son, an event which Hetty Green had never forgotten.

In the years immediately following the collapse of Cisco & Son, Hetty had set about buying as many of the Houston and Texas Central's bonds as she could, and they were now cheap as a result of Huntington's effective refusal to honour the bonds' interest payments. By 1887, she owned almost $1.25 million worth of bonds, and Huntington for one had no doubt that Hetty would be unlikely to prove a supine investor in his company.

Wanting not only to render Hetty harmless, but also to rid himself of potentially expensive bondholding commitments generally, Huntington proposed a financial reorganisation of the company. He made an offer to exchange the existing bonds for new ones, which would pay interest at a lower rate than the originals, and which would have a term of 50 years (rather than five) before the bonds' capital would be repaid. Many ordinary bondholders objected, but Huntington made it known that he was prepared to see the company fail if his offer was not accepted, in which event, the original bonds might well become worthless.

Hetty did not hesitate to make known her opposition to Huntington's plans, and refused to attend a meeting with other bondholders where those plans were reluctantly accepted. Huntington made it clear he did not care whether Hetty acquiesced to his plans or not, and the conflict between Hetty and Huntington was soon being reported in the financial press. The New York Times, which had opposed the plans for the bond reorganisation from the start, made it clear where its sympathies lay: "The Huntington contingent say they do not care whether Mrs Green assents or not; they can go right along and reorganize the company without her. Other big men have talked in just this way about Mrs Green in times past, but somehow she usually contrives to come out ahead whenever the fighting notion strikes her."

Attempts were made by a committee made up of the beleaguered bondholders to extract better terms from Huntington, for whilst they disliked Huntington's terms, they had even more to lose if Hetty's opposition led to the company's actual demise, as Huntington had threatened. Hetty agreed to allow herself to be represented on the committee by an employee of the Chemical National Bank, and went even further, meeting with individual bondholders to talk over their concerns. Exactly what she said is not known, but it seems the other bondholders believed she stood with them and would accept the outcome of whatever deal they could make with Huntington. A fresh deal was in time reached (causing the stock price of the company to rise significantly), but when details were announced in May 1887, Hetty declared she would not accept it, and no doubt watched with satisfaction as the price of the company's shares (many of which were owned by Huntington) plummeted down once more. The bondholders' committee members objected vigorously (and those newspapers which did not care for Hetty also criticised her), but there was little they could do. She was prepared to wait until Huntington approached her, which he eventually did in April 1888. Exactly what they agreed between themselves, and the price Huntington had to pay for Hetty's cooperation, was kept a closely guarded secret, but Hetty finally agreed to give her consent to the reorganisation. Wall Street observers of the drama generally concluded that Hetty had emerged as the winner.

Hetty was by now well aware of the financial opportunities offered by the Lone Star State, and was eager to expand her interests in the state's railroad companies. She had already acquired control of a branch of the

Texas Central Railway,[31] which possessed 54 miles of railroad track (and half a million acres of land), but she wanted more.

She knew too that Huntington was eager to expand the Southern Pacific system in Texas, particularly by building spur lines which would connect distant parts of the state to the principal trans-continental line. This involved not only new railroad lines, but where possible acquiring other railroad companies with suitable tracks already laid which could be incorporated into the existing network. One of the companies which came to Huntington's attention was the Waco and Northwestern Texas Railroad which had been in receivership since 1885, but which Huntington hoped under his management would provide transport links to the Texas Panhandle, and beyond, allowing access to states such as Kansas and Colorado. Inevitably Hetty learned of Huntington's interest in the company and was determined to acquire it herself.

The Waco and Northwestern was to be sold by auction in the town of Waco itself, in December 1892, and Huntington had dispatched a representative called Julius Kruttschnitt to act on his behalf, authorising him to spend up to $1.25 million if this was required to gain control of the railroad.[32] Hetty was represented at the auction by Ned, who was then twenty four years old, and had travelled to Texas from Chicago specifically for the purpose of attending the auction.

The auction began, and Kruttschnitt soon announced a bid of $800,000. Other would-be purchasers followed with their bids, but one by one they dropped out as it soon became clear that the auction was a contest between Ned and Kruttschnitt. Kruttschnitt drew gasps when he announced a bid of $1.25 million but Ned promptly responded with an

---

[31] This was distinct from Huntington's Houston and Texas Central; they were different companies. Hetty had acquired her Texas Central out of bankruptcy, having earlier bought bonds issued by the company before its bankruptcy was announced.

[32] Kruttschnitt eventually became Chairman of the Southern Pacific in 1913.

offer of $1.365 million. Krutschnitt had reached his limit and dared not bid higher, and the auctioneer declared Ned, acting on behalf of his mother, to be the winner.

It was not as simple as that. Huntington had no intention of allowing control of the Waco and Northwestern to fall under the control of someone else, and certainly not Hetty Green. He and various colleagues suddenly claimed liens over various important pieces of land owned by the company, followed shortly afterwards by the state and local governments who claimed key parts of the land under dispute actually belonged to them. Hetty and Ned argued that they had proceeded on the understanding that the land in question was owned by the company, and that they had no interest in acquiring the company without the land. Huntington in turn sought to argue that the Greens should be obliged to buy the company with or without the land, thus potentially turning the purchase into a financial disaster. The result of all this was a series of court battles which kept teams of lawyers busily employed for three years, though during the course of all this, Hetty and Ned found themselves unexpectedly hailed as heroes for challenging Huntington, especially by a group of Californian farmers who had been at loggerheads with the railroad tycoon for years. The admiration of the farmers was such that they sent Hetty a gift of a forty four calibre revolver together with holster and cartridges. Hetty, by now used to being criticised in the press and by members of the public, cherished the gift. She may also have had it in mind at later times when she liked to recount a meeting that had taken place in New York between Huntington and herself at the height of the dispute. The meeting started calmly enough, but then Huntington made the mistake of warning Hetty that he would see Ned in jail if Hetty did not back down. According to the story, Hetty looked severely at Huntington and simply stated: "Up to now, Huntington, you have dealt with Hetty Green, the business woman. Now you are fighting Hetty Green, the mother. Harm one hair of Ned's head and I'll put a bullet through your heart." The meeting apparently ended very shortly thereafter with Huntington rapidly vacating the premises, leaving his hat behind.

Whilst the dispute continued, Hetty was not diverted from the needs of her other interests in Texas, and especially the Texas Central, which was soon renamed the Texas Midland Railroad Company. It needed a full-time manager, and Hetty decided not only to reorganise the board of directors (interestingly, one of the new directors was her husband, Edward Green) but also to appoint Ned as company president. This would require Ned to move to Texas permanently, abandoning the home he had been making for himself in Chicago. He dutifully obliged his mother, moved to Terrell, Texas in January 1893, and remained based in Texas for the next sixteen years.

Ned rapidly came to appreciate life in Texas, and would later declare his years spent there were amongst the happiest in his life. Hetty had not sent him there to enjoy himself however. The Texas Midland (as it was now called) was a ramshackle railroad, with worn out track and old-fashioned locomotives and stock, desperately in need of attention and investment. Ned, with memories of Hetty's careful monitoring of him during his years in Chicago, was at first hesitant to assume too much independent control, often referring issues and decisions back to his mother. Hetty however, seems to have reached the decision that her son had gained enough experience and judgment for a significant weakening of the financial leash, for when he telegraphed her for advice shortly after his arrival, she replied "You are on the ground. Mind your own business." Another time, when Ned travelled to New York to consult her on a particular issue, she said tersely "I sent you to Texas to learn the railway business. I can't teach you by telegraph from New York. Go back and do the best you can."

Once Ned overcame his initial nerves, he rapidly proved his mother's confidence in him was not misplaced, and he later enjoyed telling reporters of how his mother had finally stood back, evincing confidence in his business abilities. There continued to be times when Hetty would intervene in his business activities; she was not granting him complete and absolute independence, but from now on, she began to allow him a significant degree of autonomy. He made the most of the opportunity, throwing himself into the task of overhauling the company, replacing track and stock, expanding the line to permit easier and better connections, and hiring seasoned professionals to run the railroad on a day-to-day basis. By 1897, the company had over 125 miles of track, and was beginning to gain a reputation as one of the most reliable, and luxurious, railroads in Texas. Under Ned's direction, the company replaced wooden bridges with ones made of steel, and trains began to run not only with electric headlights and new passenger carriages, but also with restaurant and observation lounges. New stations were built and timetables improved, and importantly, adhered to, and the once bankrupt company began to generate significant profits. Hetty quietly approved.

A significant part of the cost of all these improvements was met out of $500,000 which Ned had brought with him when he was first despatched to Terrell. On first arriving, he had deposited the cheque at the town's American National Bank. Despite its grandiose name, the bank had hitherto been a simple provincial bank operating on a small scale, and the depositing of Ned's cheque had meant the bank's assets at least doubled overnight. The bank, well aware of the advantages conferred by a close relationship with the Greens, soon made Ned a vice-president.

In the meantime, the dispute with Hartington over the Waco and Northwestern continued. It finally reached a conclusion in 1895, when the court ruled that the land claimed by both Hartington and the state and local governments to be subject to liens had not, in fact formed part of the assets of the railroad company, but that the Greens should not be forced to proceed with the purchase. Hetty's deposit was repaid, and she made no challenge when Hartington stepped forward once more to buy the company. By now, the price was $1,505,000. Hartington paid it and set about absorbing the railroad into the Southern Pacific network. Hetty at least had the satisfaction of knowing that she had been instrumental in forcing Hartington to spend at least $255,000 more than he had intended, and that her own railroad interests in the Lone Star State were flourishing.

Managing those interests, and serving as vice-president of the American National Bank were not the only matters which kept Ned occupied. In August 1893, he had attended the World's Fair in Chicago, where had seen an exhibition of postage stamps. His interest in philately flared, and he began to collect rare issues. Over time, he would build one of the finest collections of rare stamps (and coins) in the world. It was also to become one of the world's most valuable collections, so Hetty presumably approved, although it was not an investment she herself would have made.

She was less keen on some of Ned's other activities. The arrival of a rich young single man in Terrell naturally attracted the attention of socially and fiscally ambitious parents keen that Ned should come to an appreciation of their unmarried daughters. Before long, he was an important fixture in the town's social activities, regularly being invited to dinners and other entertainments by the town's wealthier citizens. He was a generous and popular host in turn, though he resisted being ensnared into premature matrimony, instead moving into a comfortable apartment block, which he shared with several other bachelors and with whom he vied in the throwing of frequent parties at which there was a heavy emphasis on the presence of women and alcohol.

Among the women who appeared, or rather reappeared, in his life at around this time was a lady called Mabel Harlow. Said by some to be a chorus girl, and by others, perhaps less generous, a former prostitute, she had known Ned in Chicago. Whether he had summoned her to Terrell, or whether she had arrived on her own initiative, is not clear, but he seems to have been pleased to see her, for he arranged for her to be housed in a nearby apartment, and she became (if she hadn't become already) his mistress. Within a year, however, he seems to have decided that Terrell was too small a community to prevent his relationship with Mabel from becoming the subject of scurrilous gossip, and he concluded the time had come to move to Dallas, which was well on the way to becoming one of the most important financial centres of Texas. It was also large enough for his and Mabel's relationship to escape censorious comment. They moved first into the Grand Windsor Hotel, and then to a large apartment at the corner of Elm and Griffin Streets and lived contentedly together. Ned, when queried about her, would introduce Mabel as his "housekeeper". For her part, Hetty at first could not abide Mabel, calling her "Miss Harlot", but in this area of his life at least, Ned was determined to make his own decisions. He and Mabel never married during Hetty's lifetime, but he did not hide from his mother the fact of their relationship. In time, Hetty began to grow a little more tolerant of Mabel, presumably noting that she made no attempt to make outrageous financial or matrimonial demands, and perhaps served to protect Ned from the attention of unscrupulous gold-diggers.[33] It cannot however, be said that Hetty ever really warmed to Mabel.

---

[33] Though that term was not commonly used to describe women with ambitions to ensnare wealthy men until around 1915.

Hetty's Empire

Important though Hetty's investments in Texas were, they only formed part of what must now be described as her financial empire. By the mid-1890s she owned scores of properties of all kinds in towns and cities spread across the USA, including New York, Chicago, Boston, Dallas and San Francisco, most of which she had acquired by way of foreclosure. Once she acquired a property, she seldom sold it or improved it, preferring simply to rent it out. This gave her a significant income stream, whilst at the same time allowing her to enjoy the benefit of the capital appreciation of her properties as America's urban centres expanded around them. She also owned mines and agricultural holdings. By the mid-1890s, her property holdings alone were estimated by some to be worth around $60 million (about $1.8 billion today).[34] Cash rich, she seldom if ever had to borrow, but was a source of funds to others, not only individuals and businesses but also civic municipalities across America. Thanks to the continuing depression following the Panic of 1893, there was no shortage of cash-strapped people and institutions clamouring to borrow from Hetty, including the City of New York, to which she lent several million dollars in the late 1890s and early 1900s.

Despite her continuing reputation for extreme frugality and eagerness to obtain value for money, she was in fact generally fair and reasonable when setting the terms for a loan unless she felt she had been crossed, when she could indeed be ruthless in protecting herself and her fortune. Borrowers were often pleasantly surprised when they realised that she was usually content to agree loans at the prevailing interest rates of the

---

[34] Those seeking to gauge her wealth included the populist Democratic Presidential contender William Jennings Bryan, who didn't like Hetty, and attacked her publicly in some of his speeches.

day. And so long as they met their loan repayment obligations, and did not try to cheat her, they had little to fear from Hetty.

She spent much of the mid-1890s continuing to travel back and forth across the country by railroad, anxious to keep a close eye on her investments and to add to them. Sometimes she travelled in the company of Ned or Sylvie, and sometimes by herself. "I travelled for two years and stayed in forty hotels" she later claimed referring back to this time. Her habits of economy stayed with her when she travelled; she was usually content simply to take a seat in an ordinary passenger carriage rather than hire a more luxurious sleeper car, as her fellow multi-millionaires most certainly would have done in her place if they had not in fact owned one outright. Although she later referred to staying in hotels during this time, she was in fact more likely to be found when away from home taking rooms in cheap and basic boarding houses, even if she owned, or at least had a significant interest in, the finest hotel in town. Her style of clothing did not alter either, and the reporters who continued to follow her around (when they could) almost invariably made a point of commenting on her habit of wearing old, worn and still sometimes none too clean dresses, frequently made of black cloth or some other dark material, and her carrying an ancient and decrepit carpet bag, in which she kept a large set of keys to many of her properties.

When not travelling back and forth across the country, Hetty still spent much of her time during the day attending to business at the Chemical National Bank on Broadway in Manhattan, though in an effort to fend off the unwanted attentions of tax men, reporters and members of the general public keen to make her acquaintance either out of sheer curiosity or with the (forlorn) hope of begging money from her, she still frequently continued to take rooms in boarding houses, tenements and basic hotels in various locations in Brooklyn, Manhattan, New Jersey and elsewhere, sometimes in the company of Sylvie, sometimes alone, and often using a false name.[35] As had by now long been her practice, she seldom stayed at any one place for more than a few weeks, sometimes only for a few days, before moving on to a new location. Even so, she did not completely manage to evade unwanted attention from others. Newspaper reporters in particular were always keen to learn of her whereabouts, and were not above bribing maids and other domestic staff in boarding houses and hotels for information about her movements. Moreover, on at least one occasion, tax officials acting for New York City tried to prove in court that she had established residency in the city and thus should be liable for local taxes; Hetty managed to demonstrate that at the relevant time, she had been residing in Vermont, and had in fact paid (some) taxes there, which led to New York's tax claim against her being dismissed. The episode served only to encourage her practice of being elusive.

If someone had wanted to track Hetty down, they might have done worse than to check the listings of the various courts of New York City and other major metropolitan centres. Litigation continued to absorb much of her time and attention, and she was in the habit of attending legal hearings whenever she could. She used the services of various lawyers, and she occasionally found herself being sued by them when a dispute arose over legal fees, for Hetty was as willing to haggle over legal fees as she was over the price of a pound of potatoes, even when the fees had been properly incurred. She did not possess a high opinion

---

[35] To be fair to Hetty, she did not always elect to stay in cheap accommodation; December 1894 for instance found her and Sylvie residing in a suite of rooms in the Hotel St George in Brooklyn, a relatively new and luxurious hotel at that time, and one where the management and staff could be relied upon to protect her privacy. On this occasion, reporters for the New York Times discovered she was residing there and published the fact (misnaming Sylvie as "Sevilla" in the process). The following day, the head clerk and other members of staff told reporters that Hetty and Sylvie had left; in fact, they both stayed on at the hotel for some time to come.

of lawyers but kept many of them diligently occupied in defending her fortune and other interests for many years. Some of the cases in which she was involved settled relatively easily and quickly;[36] others went on for years. One example of the latter was a case which she launched in the New York Superior Court at the end of 1894 against Henry A Barling, who acted as a trustee of her father's multi-million dollar estate, the estate which Hetty still firmly believed should have been left to her absolutely. Hetty had been convinced for years that Barling and his fellow trustees (one of whom had been Thomas Mandell) were mismanaging the trust, and in particular were charging excessive fees whilst accomplishing very little in terms of increasing the trust's capital value.

To make matters worse, in 1888, it had been decided that it was time to sell one of the trust's principal assets, 651 acres of prime real estate in Cicero, near Chicago, land which Hetty's father had acquired in the 1860s. By this time, the only remaining trustees in office were Barling and Hetty's own husband, Edward Green, the other trustees having died. Edward seems to have played little or no part in the administration of the trust at all; certainly, Hetty does not seem to have alleged any impropriety on his part as regards the handling of the trust, and did not seek to bring a legal claim against him. This was not, however, the view she took of Barling. By now, he was effectively acting as the sole trustee and it was essentially he alone who had made the decision to sell the Cicero property.

Not only did this proposal offend against one of Hetty's principal investment rules – never sell property if you can avoid it – but to make matters worse, Barling was proposing to sell the land for $650,000, even though higher offers from other potential buyers had been received.

---

[36] Hetty always claimed that if she was advised by her lawyers that her case had little merit, she would usually seek to compromise with her opponent rather than risk defeat in an open court.

Hetty had demanded access to the trust's papers relating to trustee expenses and the sale of the land, but Barling had refused to provide them to her. Then Barling had made the mistake of leaving his office in New York (from which the trust was administered) for a vacation in Europe. Hetty and representatives of the Chemical National Bank promptly had made their way to Barling's offices, gained entrance and overriding the (apparently feeble) opposition of Barling's clerks, helped themselves to such of the trust's assets as they could lay their hands on, namely about $3 million worth of bonds and stock certificates. These were carried back to the Chemical National Bank.

When news of what Hetty had done reached Barling, he had cut short his holiday and hurried back to New York. Presenting himself at the Chemical National Bank he had demanded the return of the stock and bond certificates. They were returned, but there then followed a series of legal claims and counterclaims between Hetty and Barling which led to a New York judge called Henry Anderson being appointed early in 1895 to unravel the various claims and to investigate the administration of the trust. Anderson's investigation primarily took the form of a series of public hearings throughout 1895 and the first few months of 1896.

Hetty attended the hearings, and on the whole, she seems to have enjoyed the process, even though she was reprimanded on several occasions by Judge Anderson for her behaviour, such as shouting out sarcastic comments when it merged that Abner Davis, one of Barling's former fellow trustees, had been committed to an insane asylum before dying (though this had not prevented him from continuing to claim expense payments from the trust during the period of his commitment). She also incurred the judge's criticism and was ordered to keep silent after she shouted out that one of Barling's lawyers was lying when he claimed that Hetty had always had the opportunity to examine the trust's paperwork.

Not content with irritating the judge, Hetty also managed during the course of the hearings to find herself being sued for slander by Miss Mary Irene Hoyt, a wealthy heiress and herself a client of Joseph Choate,[37] one of Barling's lawyers. Miss Hoyt had nothing to do with Hetty's case at all, but Hetty had insinuated in some of her comments to the press that Choate and others (who she described as a "set of buzzards") had led to Miss Hoyt herself being committed to an insane asylum. Miss Hoyt sued Hetty for $100,000, and reporters for the New York Times eagerly anticipated much excitement when the matter came to trial. Alas for the reporters, Miss Hoyt and Hetty settled out of court and the details of the settlement were not made public.

Hetty was not the only person who tried the patience of the judge and lawyers in the case. Barling too attracted criticism for his apparent reluctance to answer questions put to him, frequently simply responding that he could not remember. It was perhaps with some relief then, at least on the part of Judge Anderson, the lawyers and other members of the court staff when an adjournment of three months was decreed on 14th June 1895. After the adjournment was declared, and while the reporters were still present, Hetty dramatically rose, moved to a nearby window in Anderson's office where the hearings were being held, knelt and seemed to pray for a few minutes. She then rose, and together with Sylvie, who had been attending the hearing with her, swept out of the room without answering reporters' questions.

The hearings duly resumed after the adjournment period ended, and progress continued to be slow. Then, in April 1896, Barling suddenly died, causing the hearings to come to an abrupt end. Hetty gleefully told reporters that her prayers had been answered. "What I prayed for

---

[37] Later appointed as US Ambassador to the Court of St James. Choate and others had acted for Miss Hoyt during a six years long case in the 1880s in which she had challenged her father's will, and which had partly involved questions of her sanity.

was that the wickedness of that executor might be made manifest to New York" she told reporters. "I'm a Quaker. In just a year after my prayer that executor was found stone dead in his bed."[38] Hetty claimed a victory, and then a second one a few months later when the court agreed that Ned should be appointed as a replacement trustee. At long last, her father's money was under her control.

By now, the public perception of Hetty, primarily drawn by reporters eager for sensational stories, was pretty much set in stone. She was old, ugly, dowdy, ill-dressed, rich, mean to the point of cruelty, lived frugally to the point of insanity, ever willing to haggle, even over a few cents for the price of a cup of tea, to be feared in the investment world but otherwise derided or at best pitied. Most people who did not know her well (and few really did), or at all, responded to her primarily in two ways: envy of her wealth, and incredulity that someone as rich as she clearly was should live so far beneath her means. She was regularly criticised for a lack of philanthropic feeling.

For her part, she affected not to be concerned about other people's opinions about her, good, bad or indifferent. "I believe in discreet charity" she once said, arguing that using her money to invest in industry and the country's infrastructure was the most sensible way of applying it for the benefit of others. Another time, towards the end of her life, noting the favourable and widespread publicity gained by some philanthropists, she simply said that it was not her "way of doing". Hetty may also have felt that if she was seen to be openly generous, she would just encourage more begging letters, a problem which increasingly plagued her as the years went by. After her death, Ned publicly claimed that this was so, saying that Hetty received all sorts of

---

[38] Hetty miscalculated the time it took her prayers to be answered, assuming she was counting from her dramatic prayers at the end of the adjournment hearing - Barling obligingly died only ten months or so after Hetty had knelt by the window in Judge Anderson's offices.

requests, some bona fide business propositions, but some simple begging letters and some clearly from people who were unbalanced. Ned stressed that Hetty had in fact secretly given generously to charities over the years. He said that she "...never told of her charities, though they were many. The sums of $500, $1,000, and $10,000 which she gave away were many and there was a list of about thirty families who received regular incomes..."

As regards negative stories about her in the newspapers, she claimed she was immune to the barbs of reporters. "I have been maligned, abused and laughed at in the papers, until nothing can injure me now" she said. Occasionally, however, she would meet a reporter who portrayed her in a more favourable light, such as one from the Brooklyn Eagle, who admittedly described her as "somewhat stout", but also commented that she seemed to be "a woman of quiet and refined tastes". Another, many years later, recalled meeting her in the offices of the Chemical National Bank (where he had in fact gone to interview someone else), and stated that he had enjoyed an "extremely delightful chat" with "that brilliant and kind hearted woman." She was not, therefore completely bereft of admirers and supporters, even within the ranks of the press.

The second half of the 1880s and first half of the 1890s therefore saw Hetty firmly seated at the heart of, and in unquestioned control of her expanding financial empire[39] and Ned steadily learning the skills of business and investment and assuming more and more responsibilities, particularly within the burgeoning realm of the railroads. Hetty's husband, Edward, was becoming increasingly sidelined, admittedly still consulted by Hetty from time to time, and still playing a role within the family when this was demanded of him, but with no real remaining wealth or power and little future prospect of either. By this time, he may

---

[39] Though control of the trusts established under Sylvia's will still eluded her.

not have objected too much, for his health was beginning to fail, and he seemed more than content to spend what remained of his life in the luxury of the Union Club, enjoying the company of old friends and cronies and reliving old memories. There remained Hetty's daughter Sylvie however, and the question of what her role in life should be.

Sylvie had failed to shine in any particularly special way at school, and seems to have grown up to be a fairly shy and quiet young lady, pleasant enough but lacking her mother's natural drive and ability to thrive in the world beyond the circle of her immediate family and close friends. She seems not to have raised any particular objection to Hetty's clear ambition to train and guide Ned to be her effective second in command, and eventual successor, or to the fact that beyond explaining the basic financial principles of life required by any female born into a wealthy family, Hetty made no effort to ensure that her daughter had as thorough and widespread a financial training as her son. This in itself is surprising, given Hetty's own life of achievement, and her oft-repeated declaration that she did not believe females to be inferior mentally to males. It may be that she simply felt Ned was the more talented of the two, and that it would be a more effective use of her time to concentrate on his training rather than Sylvie's. For her part, Sylvie no doubt found herself in the very difficult position of having an extremely powerful, domineering mother, whom she no doubt loved but by whom she was almost constantly overawed, and upon whom she was almost completely financially dependent. With her father and brother frequently absent from her life, she had few people in whom she could confide. She did stay in touch with one or two friends from her school years, especially a girl called Mary Nims, with whom she had gone to elementary school, but during these later years she was frequently lonely. She had a genuine love of animals, particularly horses, and whenever she could, she would try to escape for a few days to the house in Bellows Falls, where she loved to ride.[40] These visits were only temporary respites however. Socially awkward, finding it difficult to express herself, and dressed in a plain, simple style (for Hetty's lack of interest in fashionable clothes for herself extended to a similar lack so far as her daughter was concerned), Sylvie's life during the last of her teen years was one of restriction and dutiful boredom, and relatively little enjoyment of the comforts of life.

As Sylvie entered her early twenties, potential salvation (at least of her social life, and perhaps her mental well-being as well) appeared in the form of Annie Leary who (with Hetty's cautious approval) volunteered to take Sylvie under her wing, and arrange her proper introduction into the world of polite society. This was important, for despite her awkwardness and shyness, Sylvie was drawing the attention of would-be suitors attracted by the prospect of Hetty's millions, and Hetty was determined that her daughter should evade marriage to a fortune hunter. Annie Leary was perfectly placed to act as Sylvie's chaperone; not only was she herself wealthy and very much part of the New York social elite, with a mansion of her own on Fifth Avenue, and a country home in Newport, Rhode Island,[41] but she understood the importance of Sylvie making an appropriate choice in the field of matrimony. Furthermore, Hetty trusted Annie in a way that she trusted few others, and was willing to allow Annie to take on the role of Sylvie's social mentor. After all, it wasn't really a role that Hetty herself could be expected to relish. Hetty always claimed to have enjoyed her time as a young society belle, but made little secret that she would rapidly grow tired of the apparently endless round of society dinners and balls and all the other activities with which the wealthy of that age filled their

---

[40] Hetty too was fond of animals, especially dogs. For many years, she had a Scottish terrier called Dewey. When once asked why she was so fond of the dog, she replied "He doesn't know how rich I am."

[41] Which was pretty much essential if you wanted to claim and retain membership of the social elite.

days and nights. Better to allow Annie to take on the task, so that she, Hetty, could continue to attend to her ever-growing fortune.

Also, Sylvie liked Annie and was willing to be guided by her.

Under Annie's guidance, Sylvie began to appear at balls and dinners hosted by the wealthy not only in New York, but also in the other fashionable haunts of the time, including Newport. No doubt Annie did her best to advise Sylvie how to dress and behave at such gatherings, but despite Annie's encouragement and support, Sylvie still remained diffident in public, showing little of Hetty's skills as a conversationalist, which when unleashed, could be formidable. Even so, there were plenty of potential suitors who presented themselves as possible claimants for Sylvie's hand in marriage. Sometimes these young men were obviously unsuitable, and Annie would have little difficulty in deflecting their attentions elsewhere. Occasionally however, there would be one towards whom Sylvie showed signs of warming, and whom Annie felt might merit closer attention. This in fact happened in the summer of 1894 whilst Annie and Sylvie were visiting Newport, when a young man seemed eager to court Miss Green. Unfortunately, Hetty in New York rapidly found out about the budding romance, investigated the young man's background, and promptly exercised her veto over the whole affair. The young man was firmly dismissed to seek an heiress elsewhere. Hetty was later reported as having told Sylvie "I found that your young man is very nice and proper, but if it wasn't for his father, the world wouldn't know a thing about him. He has never earned a dollar and doesn't know the value of money." She went on to add "...you shall never marry a society man with my consent. I want to see you happily married and in a home of your own, but I want you to marry a poor young man of good principles, who is making an honest, hard fight for success. I don't care whether he's got $100 or not, provided he is made of the right stuff. You will have more money than you will ever spend, and it isn't necessary to look for a young man with money. Now you know my wish, and I hope I won't hear anything more about your young man at Newport, who knows just about enough to part his hair in the middle and spend his father's money."

Whether Hetty really said all this, and in this fashion, is open to some debate; the conversation was reported as "verbatim" in a newspaper report about the affair which was published a few months later. Nevertheless, the reported comments do sound as if they could have been made by Hetty; they certainly suggest views and principles that she expressed in other ways at other times. In any event, Hetty's intervention did lead to a scuppering of that particular budding romance, and Sylvie continued her gradual immersion into society under the close eyes of Annie, and the somewhat more distant eyes of her mother.

Hoboken

Attending the hearings in her lawsuit against Barling, and continuing to build her fortune were not the only matters which kept Hetty busy in 1895. Concluding that she was attracting too much public attention in Brooklyn, and perhaps concerned that the proposed amalgamation of Brooklyn with New York, the East Bronx, Staten Island and Queens County to create the City of Greater New York, which was scheduled for 1st January 1898, might make her more exposed to New York taxes, she looked elsewhere for somewhere to live. She elected to move to Hoboken, New Jersey, where she first rented a small apartment, before moving to a series of larger ones, and from where she could travel to Manhattan when necessary by means of a regular and reliable ferry service. This was something Hetty appreciated, for she enjoyed travelling by water, and she crossed back and forth across the Hudson River on an almost daily basis. Still anxious to avoid residency for tax purposes as far as she could, she found she liked Hoboken and more than any other place, it effectively became her home town for the rest of her life.

Perhaps to her own surprise, she found that she gradually made friends with at least some of her neighbours, on one occasion nursing a German immigrant woman through the night after she had fallen ill.[42] Hetty would exchange tips on child-rearing with local mothers, encouraging their children to save by giving them small savings piggy banks, each with a dollar inside, and promising to add another to it if after a few weeks they could show her that they had indeed been saving rather than spending. She even lent small sums on occasions to neighbours who found themselves temporarily short of cash. Hoboken residents

---

[42] Hetty prided herself on her nursing skills.

became accustomed to seeing her marching through the streets to and from the ferry service, haggling in local shops and eating simple meals in basic restaurants, and seem to have accepted her.

Only on one occasion does it seem that Hetty thought about abandoning Hoboken, when the town authorities demanded she purchase a dog licence for Dewey. Hetty sought to argue that the dog was already licensed in New York, and that therefore she should not have to pay the fee of $2. The town recorder disagreed, and threatened her with a $5 fine. Hetty reluctantly paid the licence fee to avoid the fine, but then departed on one of her regular trips to Chicago, declaring that she would move away from Hoboken when she returned. Her grumblings over the way she had been treated reached the ears of reporters and were reported in the New York Times. "Mrs Hetty Green has left Hoboken and it is rumoured for good" the newspaper declared, but after a few months away, Hetty's indignation subsided and she quietly returned to Hoboken.

The approach of the twentieth century also saw something of a thawing in the relationship between Hetty and her husband Edward. By now, Edward was in his seventies and his health was starting fail. Despite the differences between them on financial matters, Hetty still considered herself to be a good wife, and Edward for his part remained fond of her, so that as his health began to fail, Hetty began more and more to take on the role of Edward's principal nurse, on occasions transporting him to an apartment near hers so she could make sure he was being properly cared for, and where she would sometimes read to him in the evenings. When Edward's health permitted, they sometimes went on trips together; they were together at the Tucker House in Vermont in August 1900 when news arrived that her old enemy, Collis Huntington, now aged 78, had died during the evening of 13th August of a cerebral haemorrhage. Hetty's reaction was not perhaps in the best tradition of

Quaker teachings and charity. "That old devil Hartington is dead" Hetty announced to Edward on hearing the news. "Serves him right."

By now however, it was becoming all too apparent that Edward too was dying. He lived for two more years, increasingly suffering from heart and kidney problems and in the summer of 1901, Ned arranged for him to be transported by private railroad car back to Bellows Falls so he could spend his last days in the town where he had been born. He enjoyed one last summer and winter there, with Sylvie attending him, and Hetty and Ned making regular visits. When she was there, Hetty insisted on nursing Edward and making him as comfortable as she could and he seemed to make a partial recovery during the winter and early spring of 1902, sufficiently so that in March of that year Hetty felt able to take a trip to Boston where she was engaged in yet another law suit. As she was returning, on 19th March 1902, Edward died in his sleep. He was 81, and the cause of death was diagnosed as chronic nephritis and heart disease. He was buried in the cemetery of Immanuel Episcopal Church in Bellows Falls, and his estate, when valued was found to be a little more than $24,500,[43] significantly less than the fortune of a million dollars or more that he had enjoyed at the height of his wealth, and a tiny fraction of the wealth that Hetty, now his widow, had amassed.

Hetty, more aware than anyone of Edward's faults, nevertheless mourned his passing sincerely. She spent some time quietly with Ned and Sylvie, and with Annie Leary, and then returned to New York and her business affairs once more. She also, perhaps strangely, given her propensity for walking through the streets and travelling alone across the country, seems to have begun to worry that as a wealthy widow, she might become the target of personal attacks. Two months after Edward's death, she acquired a permit to carry a pistol, telling the

---

[43] Approximately $730,000 today.

police officer at New York's Leonard Street Station to whom she made her application that she was a rich woman and some people wanted to kill her. The police officer asked her if a pistol would protect her, and Hetty replied "Certainly. And I want everyone to know that I have one." As she made her application (which was granted) in the presence of various reporters, shortly thereafter nearly everyone did.[44]

---

[44] There had been occasions in the past when Hetty had voiced concerns that she might be attacked, even murdered, for the sake of her wealth. She also sometimes speculated that her father and Aunt Sylvia might have been murdered, and that potential beneficiaries of the trusts established under Aunt Sylvia's will would have motive enough to encourage Hetty's own demise. Edward's death seems to have accentuated such fears, which remained with her for the rest of her life.

The Panic of 1907

The economic slow-down that followed the Panic of 1893 lasted for about four years. During this time, businesses struggled to survive and those unequal to the struggle collapsed. Share prices fell. Workers were laid off, factories closed their doors, wages declined and many people across the United States experienced financial and social hardship. For people in the fortunate financial position of Hetty Green however, the economic downturn proved yet another opportunity to make carefully selected investments when prices were temporarily low, and Hetty made no secret that this was an investment strategy that she followed enthusiastically. "When good things are so low that no one wants them" she once declared, "I buy them and lay them away in the safe. When owing to some new development, they go up and my shares are so needed that men will pay well for them, I am ready to sell." Whilst the American economy languished during the mid-1890s, Hetty made many carefully selected investments – primarily corporate bonds and real estate – rarely selling, taking advantage of the low prices whilst she could. She would have completely understood, and endorsed, the statement later made by Warren Buffett when he recommended: "be fearful when others are greedy, and greedy when others are fearful". Hetty was now greedy, but carefully greedy, stressing the importance of thorough research to enable a sound judgment to be made as to the value of a purchase, whether it be a building, a bond or a block of shares. With regards to shares, for instance, she stressed that it was important for a would-be investor to have a clear picture of "… their history, their dividend-paying possibilities and what they have sold for in the past. If one can buy a good thing at a lower cost that it has ever been sold for before, he may be fairly sure of getting it cheap."

Eventually of course, aided to a considerable extent by upswings in the major European economies, and particularly those of Great Britain and France, the American economy recovered. Prices began to rise again, and opportunities to make "bargain basement" investments began to recede. At around the same time, industrial and corporate consolidation became fashionable, as businesses voluntarily or were forcibly merged to create large industrial and commercial concerns, many of which, one way or another, survive to this day. By 1900, Standard Oil had already effectively gained control over most of the oil production and refineries of the United States.[45] It was followed in 1901 by a deal brokered by J P Morgan which saw the amalgamation of Andrew Carnegie's steel business with those of other steel producers to produce the United States Steel Corporation. Other amalgamations in other areas of industry and commerce followed, which when coupled with the general improvement in economic conditions in turn led to share prices rising as investors, both public and private, rushed into the stock market to take advantage of new offerings, sometimes using borrowed money to do so. Inevitably perhaps, the rise in share prices became a boom. Interest rates also rose, as did land prices and the combination of a share boom, increases in interest rates and the rising cost of land began to sound alarm bells for more seasoned investors. "If the currency conditions of this country are not changed materially" commented banker Jacob Schiff in January 1906, "…you will have such a panic in this country as will make all previous panics look like child's play."

Hetty more than shared Jacob Schiff's concerns. Anxious though she always was for good investment opportunities, she declared publicly that she disapproved of speculation, and particularly of stock

---

[45] In May 1911, by order of the US Supreme Court, it would be "dissolved" into 34 separate constituent parts, each of which would be a major company in its own right. One effect of this was the effective doubling of John D Rockefeller's personal fortune.

speculation. "I never speculate" she said. "Such stocks as belong to me were purchased simply as an investment, never on margin." The warnings of Schiff, Hetty and others may have served to temper the enthusiasm of at least some investors, for the rapid increase in stock prices tailed off; the Dow Jones which had opened on 2nd January 1906 at 95.00, peaked on 12th January 1906 at a new all-time high of 100.25, the first time it had closed about 100, and then rose a little further to 103 on 19th January, before falling back over the rest of the year so that it closed on 2nd January 1907 at 94.25. But prices of land and stocks still remained historically high. In the meantime, Hetty who only a few years before had been on a buying-spree, was quietly liquidating some of her investments, especially land, for hard cash. "I saw the handwriting on the wall" she later said. "Every real estate deal which I could possibly close up was converted into cash". Hetty was perhaps overstating her position here, for she retained significant investments in real estate. But she also made sure she had ample reserves of cash available for when the, to her, inevitable crash happened.

Her expanded cash reserves proved useful as the cost of borrowing began to bite, leading to Hetty receiving an increasing number of requests for loans from municipalities, businesses and individuals. "They came to me in droves" she said. "Some of them I lent money to and some of them I didn't". When it came to agreeing a loan, Hetty was as careful in assessing the creditworthiness of a would-be borrower as she was of the value of a stock. Some accused her of taking advantage of the increasing demand for money by charging exorbitant rates of interest, an accusation which Hetty refuted with vigour. "Those to whom I loaned my money got it at six percent" she argued. "I must just as easily have secured forty percent..."

Concerns about the economy continued to grow in early 1907. Stock prices dipped in March of that year, not only in New York but around the world before recovering somewhat, but money remained in short supply, and there were bank runs in several countries, but not for the moment in the United States. Nevertheless, a general sense of economic unease seemed increasingly to pervade the air of Wall Street and other financial centres.[46]

The crash happened in October 1907, and was triggered not by events on Wall Street, but rather in the state of Montana, where discoveries of huge deposits of copper had led to the creation of significant fortunes for the men lucky enough to gain control of the companies now eagerly exploiting the new finds. One of these was F Augustus Heinze, who had been born in Brooklyn in 1869, but who had become a mining engineer and made his way to Montana in 1889. After a series of adventures, and with the assistance of useful local political contacts and a legacy, he had established a copper mining and smelting business that became known as the United Copper Company. Unfortunately, some of the veins of copper ore that his miners were seeking to exploit were arguably under land owned by others,[47] including in particular the Amalgamated Copper Company, a giant mining business owned by wealthy financiers and industrialists such as J P Morgan and various executives of Standard Oil, including John D Rockefeller's brother William.

Eventually, after various legal skirmishes, Amalgamated Copper Company agreed to buy all of Heinze's interests in Montana (including

---

[46] The San Francisco earthquake of 1906 had done nothing to encourage public confidence in economic affairs, and is considered by many to be a contributing factor to the Panic of 1907.

[47] To be fair to Heinze, he claimed to be taking advantage of the "apex law", an aspect of US mining law which allowed an individual whose claim contained the apex of a vein of ore to follow and exploit the vein indefinitely along its dip, even if it passed under property boundaries and into areas of land claimed by others. Heinze, who was popular in Montana among many of the ordinary copper miners, and seen as a man willing to stand up to rich eastern industrialists who sought only to exploit the miners, succeeded in using this law in defeating several (but not all) of the lawsuits that he and his company inevitably suffered.

the mining interests of the United Copper Company) for $10.5 million, which instantly made Heinze one of the richest men in America.

Heinze, presumably very satisfied with himself, departed Montana and returned to New York, and to Wall Street in particular, where he established two of his brothers in the brokerage business. With their assistance, and in cooperation with Charles W Morse, who had formed the American Ice Company (and thereby had established a near monopoly over the provision of ice to New York City), Heinze conceived a plan whereby they would begin to buy the publicly traded shares and call options of United Copper until they had effectively cornered the stock.[48] Purchasing those shares would, they reasoned, cause the share price to rise sharply, which in turn would encourage speculators to sell the shares short.[49] When this happened, Heinze and his colleagues would exercise the call options, and anyone subject to the options (for example, short-sellers of the company) would be forced to settle them by delivering the shares which they had promised but did not yet own and thus would have to purchase. If Heinze and his colleagues controlled substantially all the issued shares, as they believed they would, the short-sellers would in practice have no option but to purchase the shares from Heinze and his colleagues at whatever price

---

[48] If someone corners the stock of a company, they effectively have near or total control over all of the issued shares of that company.

[49] The technique of short selling can be described in various ways, but essentially it rests on the notion of the short seller effectively "borrowing" shares (usually for a fee) and selling them into the market, promising that he will return the shares on an agreed future date (or at some point during an agreed specified period) or when otherwise "called upon" to do so pursuant to a call option. Such a bargain only makes sense if the short-seller expects the share price to fall significantly before the shares have to be returned. When the time comes for the shares to be returned (for example, if a call option is exercised), the short seller will usually seek to purchase the necessary number of shares at the then (hopefully) prevalent lower price and use those shares to settle his obligations.

they might stipulate. Effectively therefore, the short-sellers would find themselves in a financial trap.

That at least was the plan. When, however, it was put into operation on Monday, 14th October 1907, whilst the price of the company did indeed initially rise rapidly (from 37½ to 60), when the call options were exercised, many of the holders of the call-options were somehow able to obtain sufficient numbers of shares from sources other than Heinze and his colleagues, allowing them to settle their obligations (which suggests that the control of Heinze and his colleagues over the issued shares of the company was less absolute than they had believed). In other cases, brokers seem to have been strangely slow to contact their clients to pass on the demands for settlement. At the same time, rumours began to spread about the financial stability of United Copper, and banks which had lent money to the company in the past began to demand their loans be repaid. The company's share price began to fall as rapidly as it had risen, reaching 10 by 16th October. The corner had failed. It cost Heinze millions of dollars and led to his financial ruin.[50]

This however, was only the beginning. Heinze and his colleagues had close ties with several important banks, such as the Bank of North America and the Mercantile National Bank, and runs against these banks now began. Appeals for assistance from the New York Clearing House went unanswered until Heinze and Morse resigned from their positions at the banks, which they did, but by now it was too late, and

---

[50] There were rumours at the time, and have been ever since, that the corner failed due to Standard Oil spreading rumours about United Copper's financial insecurity, applying pressure to brokers to move slowly, demanding that banks call in their loans, and even lending some of those subject to the call options the necessary stock to enable them to settle their obligations. Standard Oil, the rumours claimed, was seeking revenge on Heinze for the trouble he had caused Amalgamated Copper Company. No definitive proof of Standard Oil's involvement in any of these matters has ever been made public, but nor has it been disproved.

the financial contagion began to spread. By 21st October, runs had begun to be reported by other banks, including the Knickerbocker Trust Company, which had also fallen under the control of Heinze and his colleagues, and was one of the largest trust companies in New York. On 22nd October, at 2 pm, the Knickerbocker Trust had no choice but to declare insolvency. Within a few days, two other major trust companies, the Trust Company of America and the Lincoln Trust had announced financial difficulties, and nine other banks had been forced to close their doors. Problems began to be reported at banks based outside New York, share prices started to fall sharply on the New York Stock Exchange and some regional stock markets were forced to stop trading.

There was no central bank in the United States at that time with the power to intervene in the crisis, and the public generally looked to the great financiers of the day to address financial problems. This meant that they primarily looked to J P Morgan, then the leading American banker, and his colleagues, to take a lead in such matters, as they had done, under Morgan's leadership, in 1895. At 1.30 pm on Thursday 24th October, the head of the New York Stock Exchange reported to Morgan that falling share prices meant that he would have no choice but to close the exchange before the usual 3 pm close unless something was done. Morgan declared that if that happened, it would destroy public confidence and that could not be allowed. After a hurried series of calls to other major bankers, he arranged for $23.5 million (nearly $640 million today) to be raised to support the Stock Exchange. This calmed immediate fears, and the Stock Exchange closed that day at its usual time.

The next day, Morgan, with the support of President Theodore Roosevelt, organised a series of meetings in his offices at 23 Wall Street with the major bankers to organise a plan to support the stock market and banks in trouble (but not the Knickerbocker Trust – after examining its books, J P Morgan had already decided that it was beyond help). The other bankers rallied once more to Morgan's side. The New York Clearing House pledged $10 million of immediate support, as did John D Rockefeller. The US government pledged to deposit $6 million in New York banks, and support was even obtained from further afield, with London banks agreeing to send $5 million of gold deposits. Other European financial institutions also pledged support.

Morgan was seen striding through the Stock Exchange, uttering words of reassurance, and he gave interviews to newspapers urging depositors to leave their money in the banks. The plan worked, the financial tempest calmed, temporarily. Morgan and his colleagues continued to monitor the situation, but then a new threat loomed in early November with the threat of the possible forced closure of a brokerage house. Panic again broke out, and Morgan arranged yet another series of meetings of leading bankers and industrialists.

The most important meeting was held in Morgan's recently completed library on East 36th Street on 5th November 1907. Amongst those attending, joining the meeting in the early evening, was a mysterious woman veiled in black. Her identity was not revealed (Morgan later claimed it was the widow of Russell Sage, a Wall Street banker who had died the previous year), but popular opinion was that it was Hetty, and in the circumstances, it would have been very surprising if Morgan and his colleagues had not consulted Hetty about their plans, and indeed, suggested that she might participate. The meeting culminated the next day with an announcement of a plan to provide support for beleaguered banks, primarily by adding liquidity to the banking system by permitting the use of clearing-house certificates, rather than cash, as a means of settling transactions between banks who were members of the New York Clearing House. It has been described as the first step in the process which in time would lead to the creation of the Federal Reserve. The announcement served to steady the markets, and bank runs ceased, for as soon as members of the public were convinced that banks had sufficient funds to pay them back the money they had deposited, by and large they decided to leave their money where it was. The Panic of 1907 was halted. It was not followed by a recession (though occasional financial shocks persisted into early 1908) and J P Morgan was the hero of the hour. As for Hetty, if she had indeed been present at the fateful meeting, she presumably quietly slipped out of Morgan's library when no one saw her (no reporter seems to have reported her leaving) and returned to Hoboken, satisfied that the Panic would not threaten her fortune.

Sylvie's Marriage

In the meantime, there was still the issue of whether Sylvie would marry, and if so, who? Since her aborted affair in 1894, there had been a number of potential suitors who had surfaced briefly and then disappeared. Some of them had been aristocrats, for this was a time when titled families in Europe often sought to buttress their financial positions by looking to the New World for wealthy heiresses who might marry their sons, and many wealthy American families in return thought that turning a daughter or niece into a lady or countess might enhance the social standing of the entire family. It was a popular pastime, so popular in fact that directories were published providing details of wealthy and titled bachelor aristocrats to help ambitious American mothers and fathers in the selection of suitable mates for their offspring. Given Hetty's wealth, it is not surprising that Sylvie caught the eye of several relatively impoverished aristocrats.

One of them was a Spanish Duke, Francesco Serrano y Dominguez, the Duke de la Torre, whose father had been Prime Minister and Regent of Spain for a time, having taken part in the Glorious Revolution of 1868 and been instrumental in the overthrow of Queen Isabella II[51] and the temporary abolition of the Spanish monarchy. Francesco, who succeeded his father as Duke in 1885 was not particularly wealthy when measured by the ducal standards of the day, reportedly living on an annual income of only $4,000. Annie Leary introduced Sylvie to him sometime in the spring of 1900, and presumably he was intrigued to learn that she was the daughter of one of the richest women in the world. Certainly, he saw a lot of Sylvie in the first few weeks after they

---

[51] An act that might be regarded as somewhat ungrateful on the part of Francesco's father, who also confusingly was called Francesco, since it was Queen Isabella who had made him a Duke in the first place.

met, and newspapers eagerly reported the romance, predicting a wedding in June. Sylvie and the Duke made no public comment, but when the Duke departed on a trip to Mexico, the newspapers speculated that he would travel via Texas and visit Ned en route. In fact, it seems he never visited Ned, and he vanished out of Sylvie's life as rapidly as he had appeared. Hetty seems not to have minded and had always been suspicious of titled aristocrats in any event. "Dukes may be all right" she later said, "but for my part, I'd rather my daughter would marry a good wide-awake newspaper reporter than any duke in the world". The newspaper reporter to whom this comment was made presumably approved of such sentiments.

A year later, Sylvie's name was again reported in the newspapers in relation to a titled man, but this time she may well have wished otherwise. In 1899, a man using the name Charles Frances Seymour and styling himself Earl of Yarmouth had arrived in New York from England. Though apparently not wealthy, his title sufficed for him to be accepted into wealthy society and in due course, he was introduced to Sylvie. Whether or not there was a romance between them, budding or actual, is not clear, but the newspapers soon decided that there was something unattractive about him. The New York Morning Telegraph went so far as to declare that he was "hard up" and in search of an heiress.

Seymour took offence and sued the Telegraph for $25,000, arguing that the article in question had damaged his reputation. The matter went to trial in June 1901, and was reported all over the world. In defence of their client, the Telegraph's lawyers made various assertions about Seymour, including that he was not in fact an Earl, that he was a failed actor (for he had on occasion sought to support himself as an actor), that he was partial to dressing in female clothing and that he had been involved in financial and other scandals so that the doors of society in England "were closed against him". They subpoenaed Sylvie as a defence witness, presumably hoping that her evidence would indicate that he was indeed actively seeking to marry a wealthy heiress.

It may be that the Telegraph and its lawyers also hoped that by threatening to call Sylvie as a witness, Hetty would apply pressure upon Seymour, or offer him inducements, to drop the case. Seymour's lawyer alleged exactly that. If so, then the hope was misplaced, for Sylvie attended the hearings, "richly and neatly dressed" according to the newspapers, sitting next to Seymour and chatting with him.

Seymour admitted he had spoken to Hetty about the trial: "When I heard that Miss Green had received a subpoena, I went to her mother and told her that I would rather drop the proceedings than cause Miss Green any annoyance. Mrs Green insisted I must continue and vindicate my name. 'If you have a good case, press it' she remarked. 'You must not withdraw. My daughter will testify, and if you want me as a witness, I am ready.'"

In fact, Sylvie was not called as a witness and the jury found in Seymour's favour, awarding him $2,500 in damages. Thereafter, he too disappeared out of Sylvie's life, leaving her to continue her life of spinsterhood.[52]

---

[52] There is something rather strange about this story. Reports of the trial refer to Seymour as being named Charles Frances Seymour, and being Earl of Yarmouth (though the Telegraph's lawyers disputed that he was, confusingly asserting that Seymour would only become Earl of Yarmouth "when his father dies"). The title of Earl of Yarmouth is one of those held by the Seymour family, who have been members of the English aristocracy for several hundred years, and it is generally used as a "courtesy title" by the eldest son of the Marquess of Hertford, a common practice amongst titled aristocratic families with more than one title of differing seniorities to their credit, and possessing at least an earldom, marquessate or dukedom. In 1901, however, the holder of that courtesy title was a man named George Frances Alexander Seymour, the eldest son of the sixth Marquess of Hertford, and who would succeed as the seventh Marquess in 1912 (and he had no children in either 1901 or subsequently so the

That life continued for Sylvie for more than another six years. Then, sometime in 1907 at the age of 36, and again thanks to Annie Leary, she became romantically attached to Matthew Astor Wilks, a great grandson of tycoon John Jacob Astor and even Hetty could find little in him to which she could object. True, having been born in 1844, he was no longer a young man, or even a middle-aged one by the standards of the time, and with a fortune of only $2 million, he was nowhere near as wealthy as Hetty, but he clearly was not a fortune hunter, and he was an accepted member of the moneyed elite. He was a member of several of New York's gentlemen's clubs, and had up until meeting Sylvie led a comfortable, relatively lazy life, achieving very little but doing little harm. When news of their romance was first revealed by the newspapers, Sylvie, Wilks and Hetty all denied it, but by the spring of 1908, it seemed obvious to everyone, even Hetty, that marriage was inevitable. Then, to everyone's surprise, in May of that year Hetty abandoned her apartment in Hoboken and moved into a luxury suite of the Plaza Hotel in Manhattan, where she surprised everyone even more a few days later by hosting a ten course dinner in honour of her daughter which was attended by twenty members of the elite. Surprise was compounded into astonishment when it became known that Hetty had not only sought the services of a beauty parlour before the dinner, but had also acquired fine clothes and jewels for the evening. Her appearance, at least for the moment, was transformed. According to one

---

Telegraph's lawyers' assertion that Seymour would only succeed to the title of Earl when his father died could not be true – it may be the lawyers misunderstood how courtesy titles work). That Seymour does indeed appear to have had something of a poor reputation amongst at least some of his contemporaries, having been exiled by his family in disgrace to Australia in 1895 for some unspecified supposed failing (almost certainly homosexuality). This does not explain the use of different Christian names in United States, if the two Seymours are in fact the same man. Though it may be that for some reason, Seymour simply wanted to use different names when in a new country. If so, the question then arises as to why he continued to use the courtesy title.

guest, she looked like an "eighteenth century Marquise", a compliment that Hetty cherished.

Why she did all this is not entirely clear; it may have been her way of giving advance notice of a potential engagement, though no formal announcement was made at the time, despite the fact that the dinner was generally considered a success. Success or not, it did not take Hetty long to tire of living at the Plaza Hotel, and on 12th June, she and Sylvie moved into a boarding house on Madison Avenue, not too far from Wilks' New York mansion. They stayed there a few weeks, then set off on their travels once more, first to Newport and then Bellows Falls. Then in October, they returned to a rented apartment in Hoboken.

Eventually, an announcement of an engagement between the couple was made in February of 1909, by Wilks' sister: "Mrs Hetty Green, New York, announced the engagement of her only daughter, Miss Sylvia, to Mr Matthew Astor Wilks of New York, eldest son of the late Matthew Wilks of Cruickston Park, Galt, Ontario."

When this announcement was reported in the newspapers, however, Hetty denied it, declaring she had made no such announcement. Exactly what Sylvie and Wilks thought of all this is unclear, but it seems that Hetty enjoyed baiting the newspaper reporters covering the story,[53] and may well have been responsible for some of the rumours that were printed as fact by various newspapers about the couple over the following few months. These included a story that Sylvie and Wilks had in fact already secretly married. The newspaper which reported the story had to issue a denial of its truth a few days later. It later transpired that Hetty had jokingly told neighbours that the wedding had already

---

[53] Around this time, she was reported as saying "Mind you, although I say I'd like to kill all reporters, I wouldn't murder them. But oh! I would like to pull their hair a little bit now."

taken place, and the neighbours had promptly leaked the story to reporters who were besieging Hetty's Hoboken flat.

The wedding took place with as much secrecy as could be arranged, at noon on 23rd February 1909, at St Peter's Episcopal Church in Morristown, New Jersey. The wedding party was small, with few guests, and it may be that Ned did not attend; Sylvie was given away by her cousin Howland Pell. News of the wedding was reported in papers across the nation, with some attention being paid to the disparity in age between the bride and groom, and it was suggested that Hetty had originally opposed the match on these grounds.[54] That may or not have been true, but it seems likely that she was more concerned about the possibility of Sylvie marrying and then dying before her husband, and the prospect of at least some of the fortune finding its way into the hands of Sylvie's widower. Wilks' age may have gone some way to reassure Hetty that this was unlikely to happen, but to make sure, she had insisted on Wilks signing a pre-nuptial agreement before the wedding took place. Wilks' reward for doing so, apart from gaining Hetty's consent to the marriage (and after all, he did not need Hetty's money) was to be left $5000 in Hetty's will. Hetty for her part gave her own form of public blessing to the marriage when she told reporters after the ceremony had concluded: "I am happy if my daughter is happy."

---

[54] The Boston Globe, in addition to reporting (perhaps gallantly) Sylvie's age as being 30, rather than 38, reported that Hetty had told Wilks that his "eligibility as a bridegroom was by no means enhanced by his having the gout".

The Last Days

Though their respective ages meant there would be no children, marriage to Wilks meant for Sylvie the start of a new life. No longer condemned to spend much of her time dutifully trudging behind her mother as she travelled about, deferring to her opinions, staying in drab boarding houses, eating plain fare and wearing simple, and often old clothes, she was now able to spread her wings and begin, really for the first time, to sample and enjoy life as a wealthy woman of society. Her marriage might never prove very exciting, but in many ways, it was an improvement over the life she had been living previously and Sylvie seems to have accepted the change with quiet relief.

For Hetty, Sylvie's marriage meant the effective loss of her closest companion. Though she saw her daughter fairly frequently, and she was in any event quite used to her own company for long periods at a time, Hetty perhaps for the first time in her life began to feel lonely. She still had her work, and she still fought doggedly to protect and expand her fortune, but something had changed. Perhaps in response to this, and wanting to be closer to Sylvie, she made an attempt to relocate to Manhattan shortly after the wedding, moving first back to the Plaza Hotel, and then to the St Regis, but after a few months, lonely restlessness prompted her to move back to Hoboken once more. To add to her restlessness and feeling of loss, shortly after she returned to Hoboken, in 1910, her beloved dog Dewey died, and her natural grief at the loss would have surprised those who thought she was only a cold-hearted financial vulture.

Sadness and loneliness were not the only difficulties with which she had to contend. Before Sylvie's wedding, she had never seemed to have even noticed the passing of the years, her natural energy and drive more than compensating for the simple passage of time. After 1909 however, she seemed for the first time to admit that old age was creeping up on her – after all, she was now in her seventy fifth year – and attending to her daily needs and business was more challenging than it had been. Faced with this, feeling tired and ill (she was suffering from intermittent heart weakness and from a hernia about which, typically, she declined to follow medical advice when told she needed an operation), and deciding she needed help, she turned to Ned. She wrote to him giving instructions that he should conclude his outstanding business obligations in Texas as soon as he could and join her in New York to help take care of the fortune.

Ned had been living happily in Texas, with Mabel, for more than fifteen years. No longer the diffident young man who needed almost constant guidance from his mother, he had proved himself to be an astute businessman in his own right, popular and successful, famed for living well[55] and playing a leading civic role, supporting good causes across the state. He was an early enthusiast for the automobile, and auto racing generally, and was credited with having made the first journey by car in Texas in 1899.

He had also become interested in politics, identifying with a wing of the Republican Party known as the Black and Tan Faction, based in Fort Worth, which sought to build political strength by creating an alliance between whites and African Americans. Perhaps unsurprisingly, it was not very popular in Texas, and faced opposition within the Republican Party itself, especially from another faction known as the Lily Whites (which largely excluded African Americans from membership). Nevertheless, the relatively small size of the Black and Tans Faction, coupled with Ned's general popularity and money meant that he had soon risen to prominence within its ranks, and in 1896 he had been named state chairman of the Republican Party. This in turn brought him

---

[55] He continued to enjoy throwing lavish parties.

to prominence within the Party across the country, rubbing shoulders with the likes of President William McKinley and other prominent politicians. There was some talk of him running for the office of Governor of Texas in the early 1900s, though in the event he did not. He was also capable of friendships across political divides, and in 1910, having supported Democrat O B Colquitt in his successful campaign for the office of Governor of Texas, he was rewarded by Colquitt who appointed him an honorary colonel on the Governor's staff. Ned would be referred to as Colonel Green for the rest of his life. Even Hetty sometimes addressed him as Colonel.

Nevertheless, when Hetty called him to her side, he responded, and he and Mabel travelled to New York in the summer of 1910, moving into a luxurious suite in the Waldorf Hotel. When reporters asked him why he had left Texas and moved to New York, Ned replied "I just dropped everything in Texas when mother wrote to me to come and relieve her of some of her financial cares." He admitted that he could not, of course, look after all of her interests, but hoped that he could do his part "in looking after some of the details".

As for Hetty, Ned told the reporters that she would go to "Bellows Falls, Vermont, for a well-earned rest." He added "I am very proud of my mother. She is one woman in ten thousand, although she will insist on working despite her years. I am big enough to do her share and my share too."

Hetty did spend some time in Bellows Falls, but before long was back in Hoboken, seeming much more her old self, and continuing to visit Manhattan on an almost daily basis. Gradually though, she began to slow down a little, and then a little more and in 1911, she and Ned agreed that they should establish a trust company to act as a holding company for many of the disparate investments which constituted the family fortune. They called it the Westminster Company and based its offices in the Trinity Building at 111 Broadway in Manhattan.

Responsibility for its day-to-day operations was assumed by Ned, though even after the Westminster Company was established, Hetty still kept a close eye on business affairs, regularly spending full days in attendance at her new offices and tracking her investments, now with the help of a small staff of clerks hired by Ned.

One of Ned's first tasks was to bring some element of order to Hetty's investments. Over the years, for instance, she had invested heavily in Chicago real estate so that by 1910 she owned over 90 properties in that city alone. Now however, the dramatic expansion of the city and the sheer size of her scattered portfolio of properties meant it was becoming harder to monitor and administer all of those properties, and he questioned whether the capital invested in them could not be more productively deployed elsewhere. Ned set about rationalising the real estate portfolio, by outright sale in some cases, and by agreeing to 99 years leases to property developers and other investors in others. Within a few months, the disposal programme had raised one million dollars, but it was noted by many of those involved in the deals that they were negotiating with Ned rather than Hetty herself.

Even if she was taking more of a back seat in day-to-day business matters, Hetty Green continued to be newsworthy, and for all her professed distaste for journalists, she could still often be counted upon for a juicy quote or two when the occasion demanded it, often made with considerable candour. "I have never bothered about what I wear" she once told a female fashion reporter, admitting that the fashions of the day often made her laugh. In another conversation with a reporter on the occasion of her birthday in 1912, when asked about her diet, she speculated that it might explain why she had lived so long, claiming that onions[56] were "the best thing in the world" for health. She admitted that for breakfast that day she had enjoyed a tenderloin steak with fried

---

[56] She was reportedly chewing an onion as she talked, and apologised for any odour.

potatoes, a pot of tea and some milk. Hetty it seems, like many wealthy Edwardians, was not averse to a little cholesterol, though she conceded that she took some exercise in the form of walking.

Her name not only appeared in the newspapers and magazines of the day, but also in popular songs. In 1905, for instance, composer Sidney S Toler published "If I were as rich as Hetty Green", which as the title suggests lists imaginary purchases and achievements that might be made if one possessed one hundred million dollars. Irving Berlin made use of Hetty's name and fame in his song "Society Bear", published in 1912, by placing her name in the lyrics alongside those of other financial superstars of the day such as John D Rockefeller, Andrew Carnegie and J P Morgan. This was followed in 1914 by "At the Million Dollar Tango Ball", written by James White, who envisaged Hetty assuming the role of the ball's dancing mistress, whilst John D Rockefeller took responsibility for selling tickets, Andrew Carnegie collected them at the entrance and Vanderbilt played "every rag encore" (though White didn't specify which Vanderbilt). Hetty may have slowed down a little, but her place in the popular imagination remained undiminished.[57]

One issue of the day for which we might have expected to hear Hetty Green voicing vociferous support, namely female suffrage, strangely enough evoked precisely the opposite reaction in her. She had recommended that at least some financial education for females was desirable, and the practical example of her life demonstrated that it was possible for women to succeed in the business world, but apart from that Hetty had little time for suffragettes or female suffrage generally. "I don't believe in suffrage, and I haven't any respect for women who dabble in such trash" she told a reporter. It may be that she so treasured

---

[57] Hetty would probably have been pleased to know that even in the twenty first century, lyricists sometimes include her name in their songs, an example of which is "Calamity Song" which appears as a track on the album "The King is Dead" released by the band "The Decemberists" in 2011.

an image of herself as having succeeded single-handedly as a female in a male dominated business world that it led her to view with suspicion women who banded together to fight for a cause, even a cause as important as suffrage. Then too, by this time, her money had made her so powerful that she personally really had little need for a vote; her dollars gave her more influence than a single vote ever would, should she choose to exercise that influence.[58] In any event, suffragette organisations who were hoping for financial support from the richest woman in America were disappointed.

For all her spirit and independence, she must have known deep down that her time remaining was limited. In 1911, she spent several days closeted with her lawyer revising her will, and in July 1912, notwithstanding her Quaker faith, in a small private service she quietly accepted baptism into the Episcopal Church, a necessary step if she wished to be buried next to her husband in the cemetery of Immanuel Episcopal Church in Bellows Falls. She continued to live in Hoboken, continued to commute across the Hudson, but by 1914, she was as likely to make her way to a four-storey brownstone townhouse at 7 West Ninetieth Street near Central Park as she was to the offices of the Westminster Company. The brownstone house had been owned by Edward Green before his death, and she now used it primarily for business meetings. The house was convenient for her, it was quiet and Ned and Mabel lived next door at 5 West Ninetieth. Hetty saw much of Ned (if not of Mabel) during this time. She also paid frequent visits to Sylvie and Annie Leary. Then, in the summer of 1914, the First World War broke out, and Hetty demonstrated her support for the allied cause by purchasing one million dollars' worth of war bonds. The New York Stock Exchange, like many around the world, closed on 30th July 1914 (though trading of shares continued "on the curb") and it remained closed until re-opening on 12th December 1914. When it did so, quoted

---

[58] Though by and large, unlike Ned, she avoided public involvement in politics.

American share prices began generally to rise as the American economy and its industries adapted to the flood of new orders generated by the needs of the warring nations, and particularly Great Britain and France.[59]

The outbreak of the world war, and the resulting boost to the American economy inevitably helped to increase Hetty's wealth, but whereas in the past she would have been eager to seek out new investment opportunities arising as a result of changing economic circumstances, on this occasion she seems to have adopted a quieter, more passive approach. 1915 saw no new spectacular investment initiatives being made by her, and though normal investment activity continued, largely overseen by Ned, Hetty was mostly content to watch the affairs of business rather than seek to actively shape them. Then, on 17th April 1916, while Hetty was staying with Annie Leary at her house on Fifth Avenue, she suffered a stroke, supposedly triggered by an argument with Annie Leary's cook whom Hetty considered to be a little too fond

---

[59] On 30th July 1914, the Dow Jones, which at that time consisted of 12 industrial stocks, closed at 71.42. It reopened on 12th December at 74.56, a rise of 4.4 percent. Some authorities however record that the Dow Jones fell during the period of closure, to 54.62, representing a fall of 17.42 points, a fall of approximately 24 percent which would be one of the worst falls in American economic history. The reason for this discrepancy is that in September 1916, the constituent companies listed on the index were reassessed, and more companies were added, raising the total to 20. When measured by reference to this new index (and recalculating the figures for July 1914 assuming the new index had existed then), the stock market would indeed be found to have fallen as reported, and some analysts estimate that on this basis it reached its lowest point on 2nd November, before recovering a little. However, in December 1914, no one was yet using the revised index (and it has been revised several times since then), so no one at the time was conscious of such a fall (although the onset of war certainly triggered various financial crises and difficulties worldwide which were noticed). In any event, the stock market began to rise steadily after December 1914 and continued to do so until November 1915, when the markets paused.

of the bottle. The stroke led to Hetty being partially paralysed on her left side, and Ned arranged for her to be transported back to his house on Ninetieth Street so that he could be sure that she was properly cared for. When the press learned of Hetty's infirmity, Ned described it as a simple cold, promising that she was already on the road to recovery, and beginning to turn her attention to business affairs once more.

In fact, her condition was slowly worsening. Further strokes left her unable to walk, and Ned hired private nurses to provide her with continuous care. Sylvie and Matthew Wilks bought a townhouse a few blocks away so they could be closer to her. She was not yet completely helpless. She was able to take occasional drives in the Park in Ned's automobile, and continued to take an interest in business, receiving briefings from Ned on an almost daily basis. In late June, when questioned about this by a reporter, Ned replied that his mother put him over the jumps every day. "She scolds me for the way I handle her affairs and says she surely made a mistake in my education or I would be doing things better" he assured the reporter.

She died on 3rd July 1916, shortly after her last conversation with Ned and Sylvie, in which she told them she was not frightened to die, that a kindly light was leading her and that she would be happy to leave this world. She was 81. Her body was transported by private train back to Bellows Falls, where after a simple funeral service,[60] she was buried next to Edward, sharing his tombstone.

The death of America's richest woman soon became known around the world. On the day of her funeral, as a mark of respect, trains operating on the Texas Midland Railroad halted for 5 minutes and businesses in the town of Terrell, Texas, paused their activities for an hour. Newspapers across the country carried stories highlighting her financial rise and supposed personal habits, some true and some not. Some

---

[60] Mabel chose not to attend the funeral.

criticised her for a lack of philanthropy, suggesting this was a consequence of her being a woman, and contrasting her with male multi-millionaires who, "having piled up great accumulations through unsocial methods", turned to "ameliorative philanthropy" in the later years of their lives. That was the opinion expressed by the St Louis Post-Dispatch; they were presumably thinking of the likes of Andrew Carnegie when referring to ameliorative philanthropy. But by and large, most reports of Hetty's death were respectful, pointing out Hetty's immense achievements in the business world. The Boston Sunday-Globe went so far as to speculate whether "Hetty Green – in a financial sense – wasn't the greatest woman that ever lived".

The New York Times pointed out that if "...a man had lived as did Mrs Hetty Green, devoting the greater part of his time and mind to the increasing of an inherited fortune that even at the start was far larger than is needed for the satisfaction of all such human needs as money can satisfy, nobody would have seen him as very peculiar..." The New York Times went on: "It was the fact that Mrs Green was a woman that made her career the subject of endless curiosity, comment and astonishment". The newspaper finally concluded "Probably her life was happy. At any rate she had enough of courage to live as she chose and to be as thrifty as she pleased, and she observed such of the world's conventions as seemed to her right and useful, coldly and calmly ignoring all the others."

And the New York Sun not only praised her as one of the most sensible women in the world, but observed that she "...contributed in the development of the country, a service not to be held in contempt."

Hetty's Will

Once her body had been laid to rest, popular attention naturally turned to speculation as to how rich Hetty Green had been when she died, and the contents of her will. Popular estimates of her fortune at the time ranged from $100 million to $200 million, but in fact it was difficult then (and now) to give a precise figure, largely due to the disparate nature of the various investments. It seems likely that at the date of her death, her mining and industrial securities were then worth somewhere between $40 million and $60 million, and her railroad and banking investments a further $15 million and $25 million respectively. Her New York mortgages were estimated to be worth $30 million to $45 million, and her real estate and oil interests in Chicago, Boston, Texas and elsewhere around $20 million in aggregate. A total figure of $100 million (about £2.3 billion today) for her fortune may therefore be an underestimate, but it was unlikely to have been as large as $200 million. Whatever the total figure, however, it was large enough for Hetty easily to qualify as the richest woman of her age, and whilst her fortune may not have been as large as those of multi-millionaires such as John D Rockefeller and Andrew Carnegie, it was comfortably larger than that of, say J P Morgan, who had died three years earlier leaving $80 million.[61]

As for Hetty's will, it was admitted to probate in Bellows Falls on 22nd July and it was simple in scope. Hetty left $25,000 to friends, including $5,000 to Sylvie's husband, as she had supposedly promised to do in recognition of him having been willing to sign a pre-nuptial agreement before his marriage. There were no bequests to charity; the vast bulk of her estate was left as evenly as she could devise to Ned and Sylvie. Naturally, there were attempts by various state authorities to levy

---

[61] Which supposedly prompted John D Rockefeller to comment "…and to think, he wasn't even a rich man".

inheritance tax charges – both New York and New Jersey tried, but Hetty in death proved as elusive to tax as she had been in life. After several years of legal wrangling, the US Supreme Court ruled that Hetty had been legally resident in Vermont at the time of her death. Vermont enjoyed notoriously low rates of inheritance tax, and Hetty's fortune effectively passed to her children intact and undiminished.

One effect of Hetty's death was to focus attention once again on the trust established by Aunt Sylvia. Under its terms, upon Hetty's death, the capital was to be divided amongst the descendants of Gideon Howland Senior, with the amount received by any particular individual determined by reference to their position on the family tree in relation to that of Gideon. By 1916, he had over 400 descendants, and genealogists found their services in demand as people tried to demonstrate they possessed Howland blood. Inevitably, there were numerous false claims which had to be disproved. The capital sum held under the trust however, was far smaller than many people had speculated, a little in excess of one million dollars, and most recipients found themselves being awarded only a few hundred, or a few thousand dollars. The largest awards were approximately $22,000 each; nice sums to receive but not the riches that the newspapers had been envisaging.

As for Ned and Sylvie, after the conventional mourning period, their lives resumed, but now without the looming influence of Hetty. Ned in particular, was eager to move forward, particularly in his private life. On 10th July, 1917, he married Mabel, Hetty being no longer in a position to object. Ned's approach to the marriage did however demonstrate he had absorbed at least some of Hetty's precepts, for Mabel was obliged to enter into a pre-nuptial agreement agreeing to abandon any claim she might have on what was now Ned's fortune before the ceremony was held. In return, Ned set up a trust fund for her, endowed with $625,000.

Ned continued as an active investor for the rest of his life, and on the whole successfully protected his fortune, even from the vicissitudes of the Wall Street Crash and the worst years of the Great Depression. However, unlike his mother, Ned did not cause his inheritance to multiply dramatically. Another difference between them was that he was now determined to enjoy his money. Sailing was one of his passions, and shortly after his marriage he acquired a yacht – named the *United States* – a former steamship which had operated on the Great Lakes. Initially 195 feet in length, the yacht required a crew of over 60 men to operate. Ned ordered renovations and improvements, which included extending its length to 225 feet, and which cost him over $1 million, and when finished, the *United States* was considered one of the most luxurious yachts afloat. Unfortunately, Ned and Mabel were only able to enjoy that luxury for a couple of years, for on 21st August 1919, slowly turning around when anchored off the coast of Massachusetts, the yacht struck a rock, sank, and was never recovered.

Ned consoled himself for the loss of his yacht by turning his attention to Round Hill, the family home in Massachusetts. Disregarding the original house, he built himself a mansion there and settled into life as a country gentleman, tending to his investments as necessary, and pursuing numerous hobbies. These included book and jewellery collecting and enhancing his stamp collection.[62] He was interested in the new technologies of the day such as radio, and established a radio station at Round Hill, and whilst not a pilot himself, grew interested enough in aviation to order the construction of an airfield on his estate. Disliking cold weather, he and Mabel bought land near Miami Beach where he established another estate, and they spent the winter months there. He remained personally popular wherever he went, and continued to host lavish parties. Unlike his mother, Ned definitely enjoyed his money, though the last years of his life were plagued with

---

[62] He also became famous for amassing a significant collection of erotica.

health problems. He was overweight, and suffered increasingly from arthritis and heart disease; problems which were probably accentuated by drinking and rich living generally. He died of heart problems on 8th June 1936, leaving an estate valued in excess of $40 million. He was buried in the cemetery of Immanuel Episcopal Church with his mother and father.[63]

Sylvie's life continued much as it had before Hetty died. Her husband died in 1926, but she continued to be close to Ned and they exchanged letters frequently. Unfortunately, Sylvie shared Hetty's distaste for Mabel, and despite attempts by Mabel to improve their relationship, that distaste continued until Ned's death. Unsurprisingly, Mabel in turn grew to dislike Sylvie, and their relationship was not helped by the fact that in his will Ned left the bulk of his fortune (about $30 million after taxes) to Sylvie, apparently believing it should remain within the family. Notwithstanding the pre-nuptial agreement Mabel tried to claim half of Ned's estate, arguing that the pre-nuptial agreement should be overturned and she and Sylvie went to war in the courts. Sylvie's position was legally strong, but eventually, she offered Mabel $500,000 to drop all her claims and to disappear. Mabel, probably wisely, accepted, and retired to live out her days on Long Island. She died in 1950.

Sylvie did not outlive Mabel for long. She died in a hospital in New York on 5th February, 1951, aged 81. Again, there was speculation as to the size of her estate, since in her later years, Sylvie had acquired a reputation for living fairly frugally, albeit not to the extent practised by Hetty. Even so, there was considerable popular surprise when the newspapers announced that Sylvie had left an estate valued at about $95 million before taxes (about $933 million today), and even more so that she had kept $31 million in a simple cash account. Even allowing

---

[63] And, intriguingly, the remains of his amputated leg, which had been buried there after it had been removed.

for the $30 million she had inherited from her brother, her fortune when she died was arguably not much smaller than that left by Hetty herself and it would seem that Sylvie might have been a better guardian of the family fortune than Ned. Perhaps she just had better advisers, though it is hard to imagine any financial adviser recommending keeping $31 million in a cash account for any significant period of time.[64]

Sylvie had no children of her own, and her will, when it was eventually found stashed behind some bars of soap in a cupboard in her New York apartment, was fairly simple. There were some minor bequests to friends or people she admired (Robert Moses, the legendary Parks Commissioner of New York City received $10,000) and she set aside $1 million to be distributed amongst various distant relatives. The vast bulk of her estate was left to various charitable causes, big and small, across the country.

And with that, the fortune that Hetty had contrived to build over so many years, and which Ned and Sylvie in their respective ways had sought to protect in the years following Hetty's death, was dispersed and was no more. Unlike the likes of Rockefeller and Carnegie, or even in our time, people like Bill Gates, neither Hetty, nor her children elected to use their fortune to endow a charitable foundation, dedicated to works for the public good, but also serving to keep the fortune intact and the name of the benefactors alive, perhaps for centuries.

But a significant proportion of the fortune, though dispersed, supports a myriad of charitable causes one way or another to this day, even though it no longer has an identifiable central hub. And it is unlikely that the name of Hetty Green will be forgotten for many years to come.

Recent years have seen a growing interest in the woman still dubbed by some as the Witch of Wall Street. Hetty's fame and reputation is still

---

[64] And of course as a result of her dying later than Ned, her wealth had a longer period over which to compound.

frequently manifested in the sensational stories that swirled around her whilst she lived, and continued to do so after she died, stories about her miserliness and frugality, her business skills, her hunger for money and her instinct for financial self-preservation. But whilst it is acknowledged by many modern-day commentators that there is at least some truth to some of those rumours, there is also a growing appreciation of her better qualities, and of her achievements in not only surviving in the male-dominated business world of nineteenth and early twentieth century America but thriving in it. There is growing fascination too in learning how Hetty built her fortune, without coming to dominate a particular industry or resource, but rather by steadily procuring the growth of an admittedly substantial inheritance by carefully selected investments. There are indeed some parallels between Hetty and Warren Buffett so far as investment approach is concerned, though his personality (and charitable generosity) is very distinct from that of Hetty. So long as people are interested in financial history, and stories of how great fortunes were and are made, Hetty Green is unlikely to be forgotten. And she would have enjoyed that.

Family tree

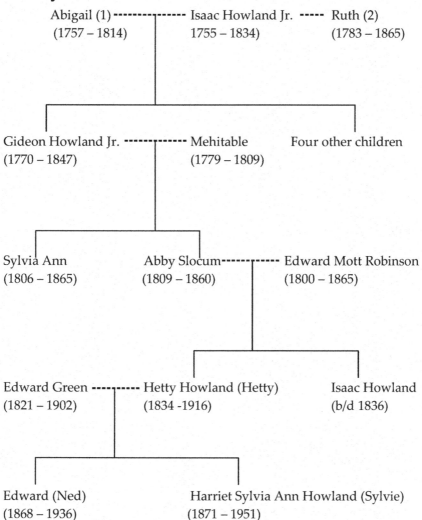

Abigail (1) -------------- Isaac Howland Jr. ----- Ruth (2)
(1757 – 1814)   1755 – 1834)   (1783 – 1865)

Gideon Howland Jr. ------------- Mehitable   Four other children
(1770 – 1847)   (1779 – 1809)

Sylvia Ann   Abby Slocum------------ Edward Mott Robinson
(1806 – 1865)   (1809 – 1860)   (1800 – 1865)

Edward Green -------- Hetty Howland (Hetty)   Isaac Howland
(1821 – 1902)   (1834 -1916)   (b/d 1836)

Edward (Ned)   Harriet Sylvia Ann Howland (Sylvie)
(1868 – 1936)   (1871 – 1951)

Timeline

Year	Life of Hetty	World events
1834	Born 21st November, Hetty Howland Robinson, New Bedford, Massachusetts	
1835		Birth of Andrew Carnegie (25th November)
1836	Hetty's brother, Isaac Howland Robinson, born and died	
1837		Birth of J P Morgan (17th April)
1839		Birth of John D Rockefeller (8th July)
1845	Hetty sent to Eliza Wing's boarding school	
1847	Gideon Howland Jr. dies	
1848		Start of Californian Gold Rush (January)
1849	Hetty sent to Friends Academy	
1859		Underground oil reserves first tapped
1860	Hetty dances with the Prince of Wales	
1861	Hetty's father Edward Robinson sells his whaling business, invests in New York mercantile firm William T. Coleman and Company	President Lincoln's first inauguration. Outbreak of the American Civil War. US abandons gold standard
1862	Aunt Sylvia's will drawn up and witnessed	
1863	Aunt Sylvia's will revised, adversely affecting Hetty	
1865	Hetty meets Edward Green and they become engaged. Edward Robinson dies. Aunt Sylvia dies. Hetty contests the will. Also invests heavily in greenbacks.	End of the Civil War
1867	Hetty and Edward marry, and move to London	
1868	Son, Ned, born	

1871	Daughter, Sylvie born	
1873	Returns to US	Series of railroad and finance house collapses trigger financial Panic
1875	Move to Tucker House	Specie Payment Resumption Act
1877		Death of Cornelius Vanderbilt (4th January)
1879		US effectively restores gold standard
1885	Moves all money from Cisco to Chemical National Bank. Edward Green loses heavily on investments. House transferred to Hetty	Cisco & Son collapse
1887	Starts substantial railroad investments	
1890	Appoints Ned to run Chicago property portfolio	
1892	Moves Ned to Texan railroad businesses	
1893		Financial Panic and depression
1900		Death of Collis P Huntington (13th August)
1902	Edward Green dies	
1907	Sylvie marries Matthew Astor Wilks	Financial Panic and depression
1910	Ned and Mabel move to New York to assist Hetty	
1914	Hetty buys $1 million of war bonds	Outbreak of First World War
1916	Died, New York, 3rd July. Buried, Bellows Falls	

Select Bibliography

Brogan, Hugh, *The Penguin History of the United States of America*, Penguin Books (1990)

Emery, William M, *The Howland Heirs*, E Anthony & Sons Inc. (1919)

Homberger, Eric, *The Historical Atlas of New York City* – by– Holt Paperbacks (2005)

Kaplan, Justin, *When the Astors Owned New York*, Plume (2007)

Slack, Charles *Hetty – The Genius and Madness of America's First Female Tycoon*, Ecco (2004)

Steele-Gordon, John *The Great Game – A History of Wall Street*, Orion Business Books (1999)

Wallach, Janet *The Richest Woman in America: Hetty Green in the Gilded Age*, Anchor Books (2012)

About the author

Wyn Derbyshire originally trained as a chemist, gaining a PhD from Cambridge University before qualifying and practising as a lawyer for many years. He has long been interested in financial history, and is the author of a number of books exploring aspects of the topic.

Index